BELIEVING
GOOD
THINGS
CAN
HAPPEN

Burnside's Journey

MICHAEL P. BURNSIDE

Burnside's Journey: Believing Good Things Can Happen
Published by Cherry Hill Media
Tyrone, Georgia

ISBN: 979-8-218-56103-1

BIOGRAPHY & AUTOBIOGRAPHY / Memoirs

Cover and interior design by Heather Ward,
copyright owned by Michael P. Burnside

Edited by Cal and Joyce Beverly, mystoryographer.com

Cover and author photos by Marie Thomas, mariethomas.com

The stories and conversations in Burnside's Journey are from the writers' memories of events, locales, and conversations with a good-faith effort to convey the truth and essence of what occurred. Dialogue, especially in scenes from the distant past, is a representation of what was spoken based on the writers' recollections.

Dedication

For my wife, sons, parents, and grandparents

*You inspired me to look good so that I would feel good
and that I would do good!*

MICHAEL
BURNSIDE, 2024

4

Inspirations

I ALWAYS WISHED my parents and grandparents had written their life stories. Since they did not, I decided to do the honors and make the effort to write my story.

I write this story because I am not only honored to have lived long enough to have something to write about, but I have been so inspired by a loving family.

I want to share how God has always guided my life, even when I was unaware of his protection. Yes, it took years for me to understand that my journey was and still is ordered by the Holy Spirit. I am grateful for the faith that gives me joy, peace, and love!

This story is the beginning of my journey, not the end. The story I have written so far is not complete, so this is just a draft.

Each day that I am inspired to remember the blessings I have been given, I will continue to add those blessings and the new blessings to my story.

Michael

Reflections

AS I BEGIN to log the events of my life, I will start with the first moments I can remember. Since Jesus forgives us for our sins, my story will not include any of my sins!

I am in a room set up as an office in a sixteen-year-old house that was designed for my wife, Cheryl, and me. The house is located in a wonderful subdivision. It took over seven months to complete construction when our home was built in 2006. Cheryl and I were so excited that we slept in an empty house on our first night there.

Prior to this move, from 1985 until 2006, we were in a newly built home purchased when it was just Cheryl and me. Since we needed more room once our sons Michael II and Wade were born, we were blessed to have a second home built.

Today is May 19, 2022. It is 6:45 p.m. Eastern Standard Time. The temperature is about 80 degrees, and there is extraordinarily little gray cloud formation outside.

My office is used for personal and business purposes, which saved me from leasing office space. Cheryl and I both needed home offices for our separate businesses, me for my accounting services and Cheryl for her non-profit for women and girls. Since the pandemic shut down in March 2020, I have had all of my tax clients electronically submit their documents, and I file their tax returns electronically. Cheryl has all her classes and meetings with her women and girls on Zoom. We both miss the in-person meetings that we enjoyed before March 2020. Although we have resumed meeting with people in person, it is not at the level it was before the pandemic. Many people now prefer electronic communications and meetings.

As I look around my office, I see warm, yellow-colored walls, a brown mahogany desk, a chestnut brown cabinet, and two burgundy leather chairs in a room that is very different from the rooms that I grew up in. This house is nothing like the government rental I lived in with my parents growing up. But I cannot take credit for the dreams that became a reality because I do not look to persons, places, or conditions for my prosperity.

I know God is the source of my supply, and God made my dreams real.

MICHAEL BURNSIDE,
1953

Early Lessons

In the Beginning
On Castle Street

MY START: My mother, Dorothy Mae Benn, gave birth to me on January 27, 1951, when she was only sixteen years of age. I was delivered by Dr. O'Perry at the University of Maryland Hospital in Baltimore, Maryland. The hospital served as a medical college as well as a medical treatment center in downtown Baltimore. My mother had such a hard delivery because I weighed ten pounds, nine ounces at birth. Mom was in the intensive care unit for two weeks after my delivery.

So, Dr. O'Perry gave me his name as my first name. He was an Irish doctor who, I believe, took a liking to me. I was named O'Perry Burnside until my mother changed my name to Michael, after the archangel Michael. She did use Perry, without the O, as my middle name and my biological father's last name. I was now officially named Michael Perry Burnside, partly Irish by name, fatherless, but an angel!

Prior to my birth, Dorothy lived with her father, Junius Benn, and her stepmother, Lainie, and her stepsister, Margaree Bailey, on 16 North Castle Street in east Baltimore. I, of course, joined this family group as a child. Castle was a small one-way street with row houses facing each other. Two to three white marble steps led up to the entrance of each house. The narrow street did not allow people to park cars in front of their homes, but it did not matter much since most people did not have cars.

The rooms in my grandparents' house were small with non-colored wallpaper, with one room and a kitchen on the first floor. A narrow, dark stairway led to two plain bedrooms and one tiny bathroom on the second floor. The bathroom did not even have a bathtub, so as children, we took baths in a large tub in the kitchen. Hot water was boiled on the stove and then poured into the large tub. It was true that there was such a thing as an icebox. You had to order a block of ice to put in the box to keep food cold. Can you imagine that?!

A small backyard led to an alley behind the row houses where we played sometimes. We had a black cocker spaniel dog named Lassie, which my cousin Leo and I shared. We also had rats, but unlike Michael Jackson, who had a mouse named Ben, we did not play with them!

In the 1950s, when I lived on Castle Street, there was segregation for adults. I say for the adults because the children of different ethnic groups did not know the difference in our skin color or care about such things. We played together undisturbed when adults did not notice, yet children still went to the same elementary school but were in different classrooms by race. I enjoyed being a child because I did not have adult problems.

The weather in Baltimore was hot, with 85 to 90+ degrees in the summer and mild temperatures in the spring and fall, but freezing with plenty of white snow and ice in the winter. I loved to play in the snow, to make snowballs and snowmen (no snow ladies at that time), but most of all, I loved to go down snowy hills on my sled. Adults would make snow ice cream with the clean snow as well.

MICHAEL WITH COUSINS LEO AND MAE FRANCIS

Me, Leo, and Grandparents

I REMAINED WITH my grandparents and my cousin, Leo Fickling Jr., until I was six years old. My mother's stepsister, Margaree, was Leo Jr.'s stepmother. Leo's father was an Air Force medic. Leo, like me, stayed with our grandparents. Lainie was Margaree's mother and Junius was my mother's father. I believe the combination of the families was God-ordained because the step and biological family members created an exciting life. I guess nowadays, it's referred to as a blended family!

Remember, Leo and I had a dog named Lassie. I was two weeks older than Leo, and it was a pleasure to have him as a sibling. Leo and I enjoyed each other's company. We did everything the same. We dressed like twins, ate the same foods, had the same toys, and traveled everywhere together! We loved to go to Patterson Park to swim.

Leo and I learned to cook when we were five by standing on a step stool to look over the stove. We cooked eggs, bacon, and grits. Granny would laugh when the grease popped on us. She said that would remind us to keep the burner low and slow. Granny and Granddad treated us like adults, I think, to help us grow up mentally.

Leo and I received gifts for birthdays and Christmas that were always alike. Even presents from other family members were the same for the two of us. Yes, we were treated as twins and probably thought we were. Leo and I never even separated from one day to the next.

Leo and I had to run errands to get groceries from the corner store at four and five years old. We were reminded to make sure the food was in bags with a receipt. Granny did not want any incidents of us being accused of stealing. Granny was very tough and stern, while Granddad was a quiet and calm man. Granny took charge of family matters for her siblings, cousins, and in-laws.

I remember Granddad and I taking long walks from Castle Street to a part of the Chesapeake Bay area. Granddad loved to walk by the water. He had epilepsy, a disorder in which nerve and cell activity in the brain is disturbed, causing seizures. Walking helped him a great deal.

Both Granddad and Granny were very gentle with Leo and me. They did not even allow our parents to discipline us. I am not sure if they just took us from our parents for those years that we spent with them, but it did not matter. I remember enjoying those times in my life!

I was often sick as a child, but I do not remember much more than having breathing problems. I had to be taken to John Hopkins Hospital often. The concern was that since my grandfather had epilepsy episodes, that I might have this same condition. Fortunately not, and I outgrew the breathing issues with no signs of any disease.

While in the hospital for a problem with my breathing as a child, I had my tonsils removed. I wanted to go home with Granny and Granddad, but they would not take me with them. I was so hurt. I did not understand that my breathing and my tonsils had to heal before I could be released. Every day when my family visited, I cried to go home. I was told that the day when I did not cry, they would take me home. I got ice cream every day! I just do not remember if I ever stopped crying before I was released because I was taken home anyway.

More Than a Taxi Ride

OUR GRANDPARENTS TAUGHT Leo and me to respect elders and others, to be honest, and to work for what we wanted in life. Of course, going to church and believing in Jesus and his Father was a must for us, with no exceptions. Religion was very confusing for us as children, at least for me. There were too many illogical answers to my questions about the characters in the Bible for my understanding. I did not understand the reason for different denominations to explain God.

Grandmom Laine would send Leo and me to church in a taxi-cab. In the 1950s, there was no such thing as Uber or Lyft. Yes, it would be unbelievable to put two five-year-old children in a taxi these days, but you never met Granny!

Granny, as we referred to Lainie, made sure we were dressed better than the preacher. She would also give us money for the church with spending money to boot.

One Sunday, Mr. Taxi Driver told us that all the money we were given was for the taxi fare. When Granny found out that Mr. Taxi Driver had taken all our money, she went directly to Yellow Cab Company to look for him. Granny always acquired the cab's number and license plate number when we were picked up. The cab company's manager gave Granny the driver's name.

Granny pressed charges against the driver, and we had to appear at a court hearing. Mr. Taxi Driver was better off seeing the

MICHAEL BURNSIDE,1955

judge instead of Granny! The judge asked both Leo and me what happened on our way to church. We explained, the best way we could, how the driver made sure we gave him all our money with nothing left. Needless to say, Mr. Taxi Driver was held accountable and had to reimburse our money with interest. Also, a newspaper called the Afro-American News in Baltimore covered the story. Headlines read: "Two 5-year-old Boys Robbed of Church Money by Taxi Driver."

Birthday and Christmas gifts were not automatic. Both Leo and I had to announce what work or chore we would accomplish to earn our gifts. This caused a profound awakening in my thinking as a child and even later as an adult. I learned to find work at home at five and six years old to earn my gifts. I would wash the marble steps or clean the backyard. As a teenager I focused on how to earn what I wanted in life. I now believe that our grandparents just wanted us to think we were earning our gifts as a way of knowing we would have to earn what we wanted in life.

Defining Two Fathers

MY BIOLOGICAL FATHER, Arthur Burnside Jr., was a nineteen-year-old military man who apparently was not ready for fatherhood. I was told that Arthur would visit me from time to time when I was living with my grandparents. I do not remember him at that time, but I do remember when he attempted to visit me when I was eight years old, and my stepfather would not let him even speak to me.

I also remember visiting him when I was seventeen years old while he was in Baltimore. This was a visit arranged by my aunt, Margaree. When I knocked on his door, I did not know what to expect. A pretty lady answered the door and acted as though she was expecting me. I do not remember her name.

"Side," she called out. That was what they called Arthur. "He has your facial features."

Finally, my father made his appearance.

Arthur was tall, very dark, and a great-looking man. He spoke in a soft voice about being nervous to meet me. The apartment was furnished with a black and white sofa, black and white rugs, and white walls with clear glass tables in the living area. I do not remember seeing any other rooms. Yet, I am not even sure if this was Arthur's apartment!

Arthur apologized for not being in my life, but at that age, I had mentally moved on from thinking of him as missing in my life.

The very next day, I went back to that apartment excited to learn

ARTHUR BURNSIDE JR.

more about his life, but he had left, and I never saw or spoke to him again. At that moment, I prayed that if I was blessed to be a father, that I would not be an absentee father. I also had the feeling that God will move people out of your life who do not need to be in your life and replace them with people you do need.

I was too young to know exactly when my mother married my stepfather, William Arthur Johnson II. I was told that they moved to a location in South Baltimore. By the way, I never referred to my stepfather as "step" because he was such a wonderful dad, and he was the dad that I needed! I would never have known that he was not my biological father had it not been for my different last name and my grandmother Lainie reminding me that my biological father was Arthur Burnside Jr., not William Johnson II.

William was self-confident, physically well-built, and assured of his self-worth. William had a third-grade education but a Ph.D. in philosophy. He was eleven years older than my mother.

My stepfather was a Merchant Marine, a seaman, who traveled the world on cargo ships. My mother was a homemaker in the beginning. Dad would bring treasures from his worldly travels, like pictures, tapes of different languages, and art objects from different countries. We were too young and naïve to understand the culture of these things, so we did not keep any of these things.

William had a brother named Johnny, who would visit us daily, especially when Dad was away. Uncle Johnny played with the boys and was very spirited and a great uncle to us. Uncle Johnny did not have any children of his own at that time. Years later, when I was ten or eleven years old, Uncle Johnny had a daughter named Deborah with one of our neighbors.

Leaving My
Comfort Zone

MICHAEL BURNSIDE, 1956

Life in
Cherry Hill

WHEN I WAS six years old, I moved from my grandparents' home to join my mother and stepfather in South Baltimore. I not only left my grandparents but also my best friend and cousin, Leo. However, I was able to visit Leo on occasions when I was eight and nine years old. You see, Leo stayed with our grandparents until he was ten. We would go to Patterson Park to swim and play like old times. After that, I did not see Leo again until our teenage years.

My grandfather would visit me after I moved to live with my parents, and I would cry to go back to Castle Street with him. I had to learn another way of living with my parents, which was much different from what my grandparents taught me. For example, working to earn gifts for what you wanted was no longer a practice.

My parents struggled to keep up with the cost of living. Therefore, children's thoughts about working for their gifts were not their priority. Even if you worked for what you wanted, money to pay you was not available. So even if you did extra chores, there was no money to pay in dollars, and gifts would not magically appear! This is when I realized that when you do extra work to earn money, make sure the person you are doing the job for can pay you!

I learned two things from this experience. One, the work that we do must be unto God, because money may not be available. The second thing I began to understand was if payment was necessary, then find a source where payment was available.

A Growing Family

BETWEEN 1957 AND 1969, I enjoyed living in south Baltimore in a community called Cherry Hill. It was a beautiful place for me as a child. I still missed my grandparents and life on Castle Street.

Cherry Hill was designated for Negros after the World War in the 1940s. The community consisted of private homes, apartments, and government housing with green grass, apple, cherry, and even peach trees. What a life, or so I thought! The place was like the description of the Garden of Eden in the Bible. Children played without a care in the world since we were unaware of adult problems.

Our family welcomed a child every two years, except for my first brother, Ronald, who was three years younger than me. My second brother was William III, then Steven, followed by two sisters, Rosa and Beverly, followed by our youngest brother, Joseph, years later. In 1962, the six siblings and my parents lived in a two-bedroom, one-bathroom apartment with a kitchen, a pantry, and a living room at 2436 Joseph Avenue.

Once Joseph was born in 1970, the family moved to a four-bedroom, still with only one bathroom, a living room, a kitchen, and a pantry at 1034 Bethune Road, still in Cherry Hill's government housing. Since some large families had as many as twelve to fifteen children, our family, with only seven children, was considered middle-sized.

After school, children played mostly outdoors until the streetlights came on. There were no computers or electronic games. We played with marbles, cards, and dice. I did not realize it then, but our games became gambling games. The marbles were pretty, round, glass-shaped tiny balls that looked like a cat's eyes. The boys would draw a circle or triangle in the dirt and put their marbles in the pot, as it was called. With your finger and thumb, you would shoot with one marble to hit marbles in the pot out of the pot to claim as yours. Once the pot was empty, each boy kept the marbles they hit out of the pot. The boys played with dice for money by throwing the dice to get a certain number to win. We would also throw pennies and nickels against the wall, and whoever's coins were closer to the wall got to keep all the coins.

We played other games together. One game was called "Red-Light, Green-Light." In this game, one kid was the traffic light, and all the other kids were cars that had to make it to the traffic light to take over and become the traffic light. When the kid as the traffic light with his or her back turned would say "Green light!" this allowed all the other kids, who were a distance away, to run toward the traffic light. When the traffic light kid said, "Red light!" he turned to face the oncoming traffic. If you were caught still moving, you would be out of the game.

We also played "Tag, You Are It." This was where kids tried to catch another kid to tap as "It." When the lights came on, signaling time to go home, that last kid who was "It," would remain "It" until the next day. No kid wanted to be "It" for the rest of the night!

The boys also played who could hit the hardest to each other in the chest. We also played Double-Dare, where boys would do sort of dangerous acts, like jumping over a wall or fence. to see if another boy would dare do it. Yes, we got hurt doing stunts that we did not have the athletic ability to do.

Attending Schools In Cherry Hill

WE ATTENDED NEWLY built public schools with great teachers. I attended an elementary school in Cherry Hill starting in the first grade. The girls wore dresses and bobby socks with barrettes in their hair, while the boys wore suit jackets, white shirts, and short haircuts. I later realized what a difference the way children dressed would make. I do not remember a lot about elementary school, except the lunch in the cafeteria was only a quarter that I never had. I had peanut butter and jelly sandwiches or I walked home for lunch.

One lunch period, each class was competing for 100% participation for all students to buy lunch in the cafeteria. I did not have twenty-five cents, so I lied and pretended to look for the invisible money. The teacher, Ms. Jones, decided to just pay for my lunch. I was so happy and unassuming about what had transpired until my mother, who was expecting me home for lunch, showed up.

When Ms. Jones explained that I had lost my money, my mother told the truth, apologized to the teacher, and took me home for lunch. I was too young to be embarrassed, but my mother was. I was just mad. I had to go home and eat peanut butter and jelly sandwiches instead of that well-cooked twenty-five-cent cafeteria meal!

Momma's Meals

DUE TO THE size of the family, our mother had to be very thoughtful about meal planning to make sure there was enough food for everyone. Meals were often donated to us by churches when Dad was not working. Mom was too proud to apply for government assistance, so we never received social services or what was known as welfare. However, my mother's grandmother, Rosa Benn, would share her welfare subsidy with us.

I remember the thick yellow cheese and the brown peanut butter that stuck to our mouths. The peanut butter was so thick that it put holes in the bread when you dared to spread it! The cheese was so thick that only a sharp knife could cut through the block, but it made the best grilled cheese sandwiches.

Momma would cook navy beans and neck bones in a pressure cooker. When money was low, we would eat this all week. When Dad was working, we had kid cereal for breakfast, ham, turkey, cheese with lettuce and tomato sandwiches for lunch, and steak or pork chops with mashed potatoes and green beans for dinner. Momma made the best pineapple upside-down cake for dessert with some real ice cream. Yes, we ate great, different from the months when Dad was out of work.

You know, I have not had an upside-down pineapple cake since my mother stopped making them! I miss you, Momma, for more reasons than the cake!

A Room for Four

The four brothers shared one bedroom with one small clothes closet and a window. We had two sets of bunk beds. Ronald and I slept on the bottom bunks, while brothers William and Steven slept on the top bunks since they were the youngest. We were nocturnal. My brothers and I loved to stay up late, until one or two each morning. Once Joseph was born, he joined us in that habit.

Because of these late nights, I had an awful habit of not getting up to go to school on time. When Momma would wake me to get dressed for school, I would get out of bed and go back to sleep in the closet or bathtub. Once I started high school, which was about a one-and-a-half-hour bus ride from our home, I would fall asleep on the bus. The other teenagers used to have fun by not waking me up, only to amuse themselves by watching me get to school late for my classes.

What a Difference a Last Name Can Make

IN THE EIGHTH GRADE, I remember my teacher having us students apply for our Social Security numbers. In those days, a child did not get a Social Security card when they were first born. I completed my application which the teacher mailed with the other students' applications.

A few weeks later, my application was mailed back to my home address with errors. You see, my father's last name is Johnson, my mother's maiden name was Benn, and my last name was Burnside. I was confused as to why there was an error. My father and mother sat me down at the kitchen table to explain that William was not my biological father, so I had to list Arthur Burnside on the line for "father." My parents took thirty-two minutes to explain the difference between the two fathers!

"I know about Arthur as my biological father," I said, "but William is my daddy, so I listed him as my father. This is the man I know."

My parents were so relieved to know I did not have a problem with it. Later in life, I realized that children can handle the truth if you do not keep family secrets. The surprises are what shock and hurt them.

Family Dynamics

MY BROTHERS AND I were close, even with our age difference. We were taught to love one another early by our father and mother. We did have different friends because of our age.

Dad did not allow the brothers to box or wrestle with each other because he never wanted us to get angry at each other. We could wrestle or box with other kids, but not each other. Ronald was the tough brother who was very mischievous and got in trouble quite a bit. Ronald was fearless and naturally built like an athlete but never did physical exercise. He had a reputation as a bad guy in the community. People were very afraid of him because he instilled fear in them. Ronald earned a bachelor's degree in criminal justice while serving a prison sentence.

William III was brother three and was dropped at birth, which required surgery. The operation left a pulse visually beating on the top of his head. This caused the school system to think he was slow, so the school administrators wanted to put William III in Special Education classes.

My mother would not allow them to detour him into Special Education. Mom was so right because William III became one of the smartest students in advanced courses. William went on to obtain a master's degree in behavioral science.

Now Steven, brother number four, was the quiet brother, very shy and introverted at first. Steven was very handy around the house. He had natural abilities in repairing home appliances and car repairs. Both Steven and Ronald had the reddest complexion, and they would turn redder in the summer. Rosa, our first sister, was also quiet at first and was a welcome addition to the family as the first girl! Once Beverly was born, we thought this was the end of the siblings. Beverly was very distant and agitated as a child. She would bang her head on her crib mattress most of the night. I never understood what troubled her.

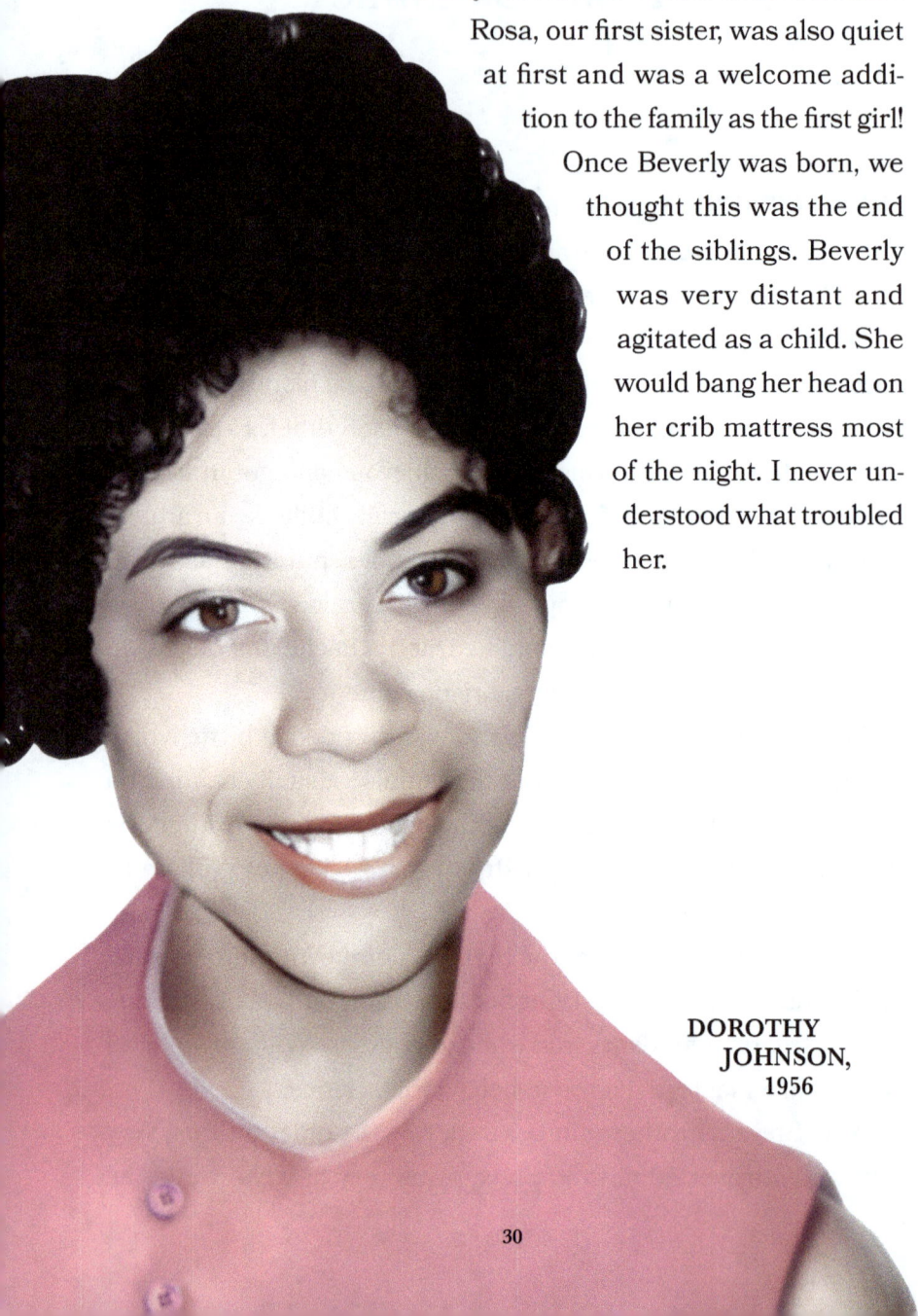

DOROTHY JOHNSON,
1956

The sisters were well guarded by the brothers. It was hard for them to date. The brothers rode shotgun over them in the beginning. We monitored their dating. We checked out any guy they were associated with. We were very protective of our sisters.

Momma was busy with the children all the time. She must have felt like the little woman who lived in a shoe. Momma had so many children that she did not know what to do, especially when Dad was away! Momma was just twenty-nine years old with six children, so she was still young. Momma was a light-skinned woman and often received compliments from others, both men and women.

I can remember going places with her and people thinking that I was her brother. Remember, Momma was only sixteen years older than me. I was not sure how she felt at times. I realized as I got older that perhaps this was not the life she wanted for herself. Momma was not a disciplinarian, except that time she beat me across her lap for ten minutes. I said I would not reveal any of my sins, but just this one time. I stole a dime from a neighbor. So the punishment was a minute per penny!

Momma was soft-spoken in the beginning. She had grown up under a dominating stepmother. I thought Momma was very passive at first, but, oh, how that changed as we got older! Momma did the very best she could once there were six of us in a two-bedroom row house. With only two children of my own, I cannot imagine how she managed to get any time for herself. I now understand her a great deal more. I just did not realize that she never had a life of her own.

Later in life, Momma became very tough. When life would beat up on her, Momma began to fight back. She still remained sweet, but you could no longer say or do anything to her without the proper response. You had to be careful how you spoke to her because she would snap back.

Even with the last name of Burnside, I was a Johnson. I could have been called Burnside Johnson.

Turning Points

Choices That Kept Me Safe
And Steered Me Toward A Career

THE SCHOOLS IN THE community allowed after-school recreation for the teenagers, and I participated in that. We played baseball, basketball, and pool at the school from seven to nine in the evening on weekdays. I had several friends my age and we would play at the recreation center together. My main two friends were Michael Brown, known as Mikey, and Bernard Scott, known as Brother. We not only met and played at the recreation center, but we also played in each other's homes as well. Mikey, Brother, and I separated as we got older. Our life choices were different, and I went in another direction.

I was around twelve years old when I found a way to earn money from neighbors in the community. Most people did not have cars and grocery stores were a distance away from their homes. I made a wooden wagon to carry their packages from the store to their house. I charged 35 to 50 cents for the service and made pretty good money, I guess because I cannot remember how much money I made. The amount did not matter, just the fact that I found a way to work and buy some things I wanted.

I remember when I was fifteen years old, shooting dice in the projects with six other teenagers. A middle-aged female social worker approached us to ask if any of us wanted to work for the summer. The other kids thought she was from the police department. They thought if they gave her their name and address, she

More Than Work in SS Summer J[

Some 500 Baltimore youngsters who returned to school last week have mixed feelings about whether they really left the classroom.

These are the youngsters who worked at the Social Security Administration during the summer under the Youth Opportunity Campaign. For them summer was a combination of on-the-job training, classroom activity and special projects that meant a bit of learning without the regimentation of school.

"I thought I would be running a copy machine or maybe would be a glorified office boy—bringing coffee to the other employees and that kind of thing" said Tom Campbell, a St. Paul School for Boys senior. "I never expected to get involved as much as I did in other activities."

TOM ADMITS that his job as a micro-film file clerk in the bureau of data processing and accounts was not the most exciting in the world, "bot you" realize that its important and that somebody has to do it," he added.

His real thrill, he asserts came from his participation in a discussion group on current events, and a reading enrichment class.

The Youth Opportunity Campaign, started in 1965, is designed to provide "meaningful" jobs to youngsters are 16-21 primarily to enable them to remain in school. About 500—more than twice as many as last year — worked in Social Security's Baltimore offices, and some 2,232 worked for Social Security nationwide, a third more than the goal originally set. The word "meaningful" is the key to the program as it operates at Social Security. Social Security officials have interpreted the "meaningful" to mean useful to the agency and a job that enhances the work experience of the trainee.

Courses designed to supplement the work experience were provided in remedial reading, reading enrichment, math, English, typing and psychology. The trainees attend such classes voluntarily on the basis of diagnostic testing which they were subjected to at the beginning of the summer work.

"WE TRY TO make sure every person has a chance to attend at least one of the courses," said Mrs. Barbara LeCroy, coordinator of the supplemental activities. "The idea is to try to make their summer's work as interesting and informative as possible. While their jobs mean a lot in terms of money, these extra activities can be a big help at their ... lives ... in helping them brush up for the school year, or in helping them make up their minds about future careers," she said.

The role of educational institution is not entirely new to Social Security. The division of training and career development provides courses and counseling to the agency's regular employes as well as training in program operations.

Additionally, courses are provided after hours in conjunction with Baltimore County High Schools, the University of Maryland and George Washington University.

Adapting the agency's educa-

POLITICKING was included in the summer program as trainees participated in a mock political convention. Participants included (left to right) Gregory Gordon as Gov. W[ ] Michael Burnside as Hubert [Hum]phrey and Pat Baskerville as Rockefeller.

tional facilities to the demands of ... the Youth Opportunity Campaign was aided somewhat by another special employment program, the Student Assistant Program.

Under this program, bright young college students are hired each summer. This year several of them taught classes, and a number of them served as chaperones on outings, as "big brothers" and "big sisters" during the summer.

"IT WAS A two-way street," said Ignacious Toner, a University of Scranton senior who taught a course in psychology. "I think we learned as much from them as they learned from us."

The instruction was headed up by Miss Maria Campbell, a Mor-

... graduate and Fulbright Schol[ar] ... who will be studying ... this year. Miss Campbell assert[s] ... idual help and guidance ...

Judge Harr[
Links Crim[
Dope Traff[

By MARGARET PHELPS

'The average citizen has not the slightest ... hension of the extent of the narcotics traffi[ ] ... and the huge number of crimes whi[ ]

would send the police to arrest them.

"Yes, I want to work for the summer," I said. I realized that if the police came to my house, so what? I would not be playing dice or gambling.

While some of my friends either worked outdoors on lawns or did not work at all that hot summer, I worked indoors at the Social Security Administration. You see, it takes faith to be fearless and believe that great things can happen to you.

I started high school in September 1966 as a tenth-grade sophomore at Forest Park High School in Baltimore. I was continuing as a business student from junior high school. I chose to pursue business because, in the eighth grade I started to like girls. When the school counselor asked the students whether they wanted to pursue a college prep, vocational, or business career, I did not know which.

Later as we walked back to the counselor's office, I noticed a classroom with all girls.

"What is that class pursuing?" I asked the counselor.

"That's a business class," the counselor said. "They are pursuing a Business Curriculum. They must take shorthand, typing, marketing, and finance. Why?"

"Well, that is what I want," I said. Now, it was not the courses that motivated me. It was the girls.

I learned to type on a manual typewriter which required the use of correction tape if you made errors. I learned shorthand, but not enough to remember how to use it. Besides, it was rare for a male to be hired as a secretary. Males were supposed to take shop classes to learn how to make things with their hands. Females were expected to learn secretarial and homemaker skills.

I did not want to make anything with my hands. I needed them for other tasks. Besides, I discovered that girls liked men with soft hands!

The Changing Cherry Hill

LIFE IN CHERRY HILL began to change for me as a teenager, and not for the better. My world changed, starting with the bullying I received in elementary and middle school and even after school on the street. Fighting to survive became a way of getting through a day. I had such a quick temper.

"Anger without power was useless," my father told me, meaning that anger alone does not get you your way. Dad taught me not to get angry but instead to get what you were after!

Dad had to teach me to be fearless. I had a fear of everything. You name it, I was afraid of it. That included a fear of fighting, a fear of the neighborhood, a fear of living, and even a fear of being afraid. I was taught in church that if someone hits you, then you should turn your other cheek for them to hit., but Dad taught me that meant to turn the other cheek of the person that hits you, not your cheek! This is if you want to stop being hit and bullied.

Once Dad got the fear out of me, death did not scare me anymore. Turning other's cheeks stopped the bullying as well. See, this is what I meant when I said Dad had a Ph.D. in psychology.

The beautiful Cherry Hill community that I had known as a child changed by 1966 to what many considered a ghetto. The green grass became brown dirt, while the fruit trees became bare, with no possibility of growing fruit again. Drugs and crime became the activity of each day for teenagers while parents were busy earning a living.

I did not realize it at that time, but church, school, and work kept me too busy to participate in the negative activities in the community. It was hard not being accepted by my peers and labeled as different. I understood right from wrong, yet I missed being with them. But I saw them drinking, using drugs, stealing cars, and breaking into others' property, and I not only knew better, but I was also afraid of the consequences. I saw first-hand kids my age dying young, getting criminal records, and being incarcerated. Something in my subconscious guided and directed me to focus. I know now that God guided my steps.

My mother's uncle and her grandfather were sharecroppers who tended cotton and tobacco fields. I only visited them for a short time, but it showed me how life could be lived in a more focused way. Life was much different in the country than in the city. My great-uncles, aunts, cousins, and even my great-granddad had to plant as well as grow their food. Farm work was very hard for me, but it took me back to what my grandparents taught me: how to work for what you wanted. But I still could not imagine working on a farm.

I also visited New York with my mother's brother, Willie Benn, an illegal numbers runner. Uncle Willie was a hustler who collected people's bets on what the number of the day would be. Today, this is called the lottery, and it is only legal because it is legislated by the states. My Uncle Willie wanted me to get a college education to pursue a purposeful career to better my chances in life.

These visits to these different environments opened my eyes to better possibilities for my life. I began to understand that exposure is one of the keys to success, based on the theory that if you can see it, you can be it.

CHERRY HILL

Mindless Games That Misdirected My Journey

MY FRIENDS SYLVESTER and Stanley were running buddies I met in the fast-food restaurant where I worked after school. We worked together as well as partied together. At some point, the three of us decided to be foolish by attending parties for teenagers in different parts of Baltimore when their parents were not home. There were many underage teenagers like us at these parties. My friends and I would collect money to get alcohol, but instead of returning to the parties, we would just keep the money. I guess we did it one too many times because some guys knew who we were after a while.

Then, one day, it happened. I was getting off work from the mall when a couple of the guys saw me waiting for a bus. I was in a different part of town than where I lived when I heard gunshots and two guys running toward me.

"There is one of the guys that took our money!" I heard them shouting.

I ran for my life. I had not thought of the consequences of my actions when we were taking money under false pretenses. After that day, word got out that the three of us, Stanley, Sylvester, and I, were being hunted. These guys were looking to hurt us.

My problem was that I did not know who these guys were or what they looked like. Now, fear was my everyday companion. I was afraid when I went to school, I was afraid when I went to work, and I ran everywhere I went! That's when the three of us decided to enlist in the military to get off the streets, but only Stanley and I eventually joined. Sylvester pretended to join but did not. Stanley joined the Army. I joined the Marine Corps because I have always loved their uniforms. I thought the Marine Corps was the best way to escape my immediate surroundings and those guys who were chasing me.

In November 1968, I was seventeen and six months away from graduating from my senior year of high school. However, I had to decide whether to continue with twelfth-grade activities or to leave immediately to join the military. I thought I had completed all the required course credits to graduate, so I decided to enlist.

For me to enlist at seventeen without having graduated from high school, I had to get a parent's signature. Since my father was on the high seas, my mother had to give her permission. This was in November 1968 during the Vietnam War, so Momma was not willing to sign me over to war. I was desperate and begged her to agree. To make her feel guilty, I told Momma that if she did not sign, she would be responsible for me getting killed on the streets since threats had been made to my life by some gun-toting bad guys.

I sounded like Jodie from the movie "Babyboy," who told his mama that if she put him out of her house, she would be responsible for him being killed. After my threat, Momma signed!

I had to wait until March 1969 to be inducted.

MICHAEL BURNSIDE,
1969

The Military
And Me

———◦○◦◁▷◦○◦———

Oorah!

"YOU CAN RUN, BUT YOU CAN'T HIDE."

Have you ever heard this saying? It means that wherever you go, you carry yourself with you! Sometimes, you run away from danger right into something else just as dangerous.

My mother was right. I ran, but I could not hide from running away. I entered the Marine Corps in March 1969 during the Vietnam conflict, as some called it, but it was a war!

As a high school senior, I was supposed to graduate in June 1969, but I was running, so I did not stay to march with my fellow seniors. I later learned that I was not awarded my diploma even though I had all my high school credits.

I went to Parris Island, South Carolina, for basic training as a recruit. The drill instructors, or DIs, as they were called, were ruthless and mean. These guys had been in wars and did not play about training for war. They would cuss, bite you, talk negatively about your mother, and treat you like a girl. The DIs boarded the bus once we arrived on the base, then hurriedly rushed us off the bus. If we were not moving fast enough, we were thrown off by force.

We had to line up on a chalk line in a hurry. In fact, everything from that day on was in a hurry. Now mind you, it's 2:43 a.m., windy, with 43 degrees of cold winter weather. The recruits had to listen to the spiel about Marines being the best and most disciplined fighting machines in all the military.

At 4:47 a.m., we were still standing by the beds, known as racks.

Finally, we were allowed to go to bed. Then, around 5:30 a.m., we heard loud voices and yelling with DIs pulling us up out of our beds. Well, it takes a lot more noise than that to get me away from my sleep. Remember, I would find a place to sleep, but there was no tub or closet for me to go to. I did not get up until the thin mat that I was sleeping on was turned upside down with me underneath while a DI jumped up and down on me, yelling with profanity. That was the last time I did not get up when the lights came on! I realized that I was not home with Dad and Momma allowing me to get away with my antics. I have no idea how I was able to complete that difficult training.

Parris Island Marine Corps Base had three battalions. I was in the Second Battalion, Platoon 244. The recruits were housed in barracks that had four separate squad bays with a platoon in each. Each platoon had eighty to ninety recruits.

Training was nine weeks long unless you failed any of the weeks' training. If you failed a training, you would have to repeat that week. We all stood up every day, all day. When we were in the barracks, we stood by our racks and read the manual of general orders that we had to learn and memorize. Every moment was planned but subject to change. We also ran everywhere we traveled, never riding in a vehicle. Mealtime was timed. Everything was timed, with us feeling like we were being rushed.

The first order was to get us in physical shape. We exercised constantly throughout the day. We learned to march as one in step with each other. Then we were trained to function as a team. When one messed up, we all messed up, and we were all punished together. We learned to use explosives and became marksmen with M14 and M16 rifles. We had to endure being exposed to tear gas unexpectedly. We learned hand-to-hand combat. This was the beginning of preparing us for war, but I still was not thinking of the real possibility that I would ever be going to war.

You see, I was praying to just get through the training to get back to the home I ran away from. Being in the military made me more afraid than I was on the street. Now I felt trapped!

After a couple of weeks, we finally got the opportunity to call home. My father was still on a ship in another country, but I was able to speak with my mother.

"Momma, you must get me out of the Marine Corps," I said. "They are crazy and trying to kill me."

"They are trying to kill you just like somebody on the streets of Baltimore was trying to kill you," Momma said. "I can't get you out. You will have to live with it."

It did not dawn on me the pain that I had put my mother through, and now I was doing it again by telling her I felt that my life was in danger. You see, parents bear the pain of their children growing up, always worrying for their safety even after the child is grown. Of course, I did not realize this until I had children much later in life.

I completed my training in nine weeks and graduated from being a Marine recruit to being a Private First Class Marine in July 1969. I was sent to Camp LeJeune, North Carolina, for two months of infantry training, which involved jungle warfare engagement. There was more hand-to-hand combat with more weapons and in-depth explosive training.

Training involved camping in the woods for days at a time to learn how to live in a jungle setting. The gear you carried was your rifle, some clothes, and food in cans known as C-rations packed in a backpack. I felt like I was having an out-of-body experience. I was going through the motion of training, but my heart was focused on how to get back home safely.

After the Infantry training, I was able to go home to Baltimore for two weeks. My next military assignment was Camp Pendleton, California, for the final preparation for Vietnam. The world I arrived home to confused me. Most of my friends were gone, taken either by death, drugs, or prison, within about four months of my leaving. I could not put the pieces together because I was so heartbroken. I believe that being away from the neighborhood spared me from becoming a negative statistic like my friends.

I cannot remember much about what I did on my two-week vacation before going to California. My thoughts were about going to a foreign country to fight people I did not know and who had not done anything to me. What a life–to live in a country where prejudice and racial divide were based on the color of your skin. A country where my ancestors were slaves, yet I was expected to put my black butt at risk for a cause that I did not understand. I could not figure out what was worse–the condition of my community and friends or going off to war in a foreign country.

I left for Camp Pendleton in late July 1969, uncertain if I would ever return home again. I sadly said my farewells to my family with no thoughts of returning. My mother did not let on what her feelings were about me heading for war. Once I arrived on the base, I was once again housed in a barracks with four squad bays. Now as a Marine and not a recruit, it was different from how we were treated. We no longer had to act subservient to higher-ranking Marines.

My background in business allowed me to be a 0141 Office Marine and a 0161 Postal Marine. Yet regardless of your duties, every Marine was a grunt, a fighting machine. That was the main training we received. I met other Marines from different U.S. cities and some of us became friends.

However, as the training and preparation to go to Vietnam continued, I began to understand the seriousness of going to war. I saw men returning from the war with missing limbs or experiencing mental issues. For the first time in my life, I experienced real notable prejudice from white people on and off the military base.

Decision to Prevent Going to Vietnam

I WATCHED AS SOME MARINES completed their training and left for their tour in Vietnam. I also watched as some of the men found ways to avoid going to war by acting insane or shooting themselves in the foot. Literally, it appeared that none of those antics worked. They still were shipped out for war.

I realized that I could not go to war, nor could I fight for a country that did not accept me as human. I was determined that I would not go to war. I saw in my mind what I needed to do. I first wrote to Richard Nixon, who was president of the United States at that time, asking for a waiver as the oldest son. I did receive a response to my letter on behalf of the president. The letter corrected my thinking about the rule, which had nothing to do with the oldest son but rather the only son to carry on the family's last name.

Next, I went to the military chaplain to plead as a religious conscientious objector. The chaplain told me that most wars were religious wars, so that did not prevent me from going to the battleground. Then, I tried pleading my case with the commanding officers who were pro-war. They just laughed at me.

Finally, I decided there was no use talking or explaining to anyone why I was determined not to go to war. So, I stopped talking to my military friends and my family. I stopped writing letters or communicating in any way to anyone.

After weeks of not talking, the base commander had the military police escort me to my meals daily. I would still make formation, exercise with the troops, and perform my duties. I just was not talking.

Finally, I was escorted to the commander's office. The commander first sent me to the naval hospital to meet with a naval psychiatrist. The psychiatrist was not pleased with me because he could not make sense of why I was not speaking. I was returned to my duty station with the commanding officer, labeled as non-responsive.

Once I arrived back with the commanding officer, I was told that if I disobeyed his order to speak, I would be sent to military prison. Well, the cat got my tongue, and I just could not speak! So, I was locked up in the brig. After a week in the brig, a captain visited me in my cell. The captain told me that he was not sure why I could not or would not speak, but he was sure that my not speaking was not a crime.

Therefore, he returned me to my duty station. I was given duties on the base at Camp Pendleton, California, where I remained until late November 1970, when I was honorably discharged from the Marine Corps.

Yes, that's right. I did not talk for months until I was honorably discharged. This, for me, was the power of prayer and determination. It taught me that no one can make you do what you are not willing to do, but there are consequences.

What are you willing to sacrifice?

MICHAEL BURNSIDE, 1969

BALTIMORE CITY HALL

Back to Baltimore

Returning to
"The World"

I ARRIVED IN BALTIMORE on November 20, 1970, with no plans for what I would do. I rejoined to "the world," as Marines used to call it when you leave military life. "The world" was different than I remembered. I came home to streets full of sounds by Marvin Gaye, *What's Happening Brother?* That whole album told the story of what was happening in "the world" that I found myself part of.

I first decided to visit Uncle Willie Benn, my mother's younger brother, in New York City to see if I could change my circumstances. But the streets were the same as in Baltimore. There was no hope for betterment in New York. Therefore, I returned to Baltimore.

I did not know where I planned to live or work or even what I was going to wear outside of the Marine Corps clothing. When an active Marine becomes a veteran, he becomes a civilian and is on his own. He must fend for himself. He must pay for shelter, food, and clothing, all of which were previously paid for by the government. I was no longer being sponsored by the military.

Of course, with no plans, I landed back with my parents and my siblings. Everyone was excited to see me still alive without any orders to go to Vietnam. However, I now needed a job. I only had business skills, and I discovered that I did not even have a high school diploma!

With nothing to do, I turned to what I knew, which was exercise. I was accustomed to staying in shape, so every day, I would put on a backpack with a radio on my back and run five to ten miles. I also started martial arts training.

The Cherry Hill community I returned to was now even worse than when I first left. The crime rate had increased tremendously. My former friends were either using drugs, imprisoned, or murdered in the streets. Ironically, going into the military saved me from a terrible way of life. Now, I just needed to ensure I was mature enough not to follow the path of destruction!

An Important Break-Up

I MET CAMILLE while attending Forest Park High School in Baltimore. It was strange how a schoolmate of mine, Camille, and her friend Rose, ended up at Forest Park High School's junior prom dance in 1968. I do not remember all the details, but I do remember my schoolmate who was driving took the four of us to a McDonald's fast-food restaurant after the dance.

Later, when we were back in school, some students laughed at my buddy and me for taking our dates to McDonald's. The funny thing was that I did not realize that Camille and Rose were our dates. We just happened to leave the dance at the same time.

Anyway, I reconnected with Camille after I was discharged from the Marine Corps in 1970. Camille and I dated for as long as she could tolerate my foolishness.

You see, I wasn't clear on what my goals were nor what I wanted in life yet. I played the street games that I had learned in my environment, but Camille had definite goals and a focus for her life. So, while I was playing and working meaningless jobs, Camille was going to college and was engaged in meaningful employment.

One day, Camille would not answer my phone calls. (This was before cellphones.) I decided to just visit her at her parents' home. It just so happened that Camille and a male friend were coming out of the house. The friend opened his car door to let Camille get in the passenger seat. By the way it was a nice little sports car, and I did not own a car!

Camille would not talk to me then, but when she finally did talk to me, it was to tell me that she had a new friend and that I was not moving in the right direction. Of course, I tried to talk her into giving me another go at it, but she could not because it went against her morals. Finally, I realized that this was one of God's lessons he gave me.

You see, after Camille, I met women who just wanted to party without any thought of the future, without goals for what they wanted in life. I now prayed that if God would give me another chance with a woman who had plans for a fantastic future, that I would be a better man. Later, God answered my prayers and introduced me to the woman I prayed for.

Determined To
Change My Direction

IN 1971, I DECIDED TO CHANGE MY ENVIRONMENT. I left my parents' home without another place to go. I stayed in hotels, slept in cars, or visited old friends late at night to sleep over. Basically, I was homeless! I decided to change my situation. After all, I had nothing to lose by trying.

I started with the State of Maryland Social Services, looking for financial assistance since I was homeless. I was first told by one of the social services employees that I was a lazy dude attempting to milk the state instead of getting a job. Fortunately, I had pay stubs from jobs and the military that showed I had not only worked but paid state and federal taxes. After I showed the pay stubs and convinced the employee that I was a veteran, he decided to help me. The employee explained that because I was homeless, he could only get me a one-time payment. That was all I needed for a start.

I challenged myself to get a General Education Diploma (GED), and I did. I passed the exam on the first try. I have no idea how. Even with the GED, jobs were hard to obtain. I was just another unemployed veteran with no skills, no job, and no plans.

I was able to get a job with the main U.S. Post Office in Baltimore during the winter holidays. I first worked sorting letters by ZIP Code. In this position, you were timed by how fast you could sort the letters into a slot. A supervisor, known as a floor walker, watched and timed your every move, including when you talked to co-workers. Breaks to the bathroom were timed, and we were given only 30 minutes for lunch.

I was reassigned to load and unload mail from tractor-trailer trucks. The work was overwhelming. I had to do something else to keep my sanity. Maybe, I thought, I need to get an education to earn a specific skill!

So, I enrolled in an accounting program at a two-year private college, Bay College of Maryland, since they accepted my GED diploma. You see, some colleges only accept high school diplomas.

I attended college full-time while driving a taxicab to earn money. However, I only made enough to pay for the rental of the taxi and gas. This was called "making your nut." The great thing about driving the cab, even without making money, is that the cab served as transportation since I did not have a vehicle.

Meanwhile, I still did not have a place to live. If your name is not on a lease, then you are considered homeless!

The VA Was
Forced to Help

MY NEXT STOP was visiting the Veterans Administration (VA) for that much needed help I discussed! The administration director sent me to the VA Hospital since I was homeless to see if I could be accepted into a VA program there. I had to be interviewed by the director of the program to determine if I was eligible.

The director referred me to a psychiatrist to help me, since he could not, or so he thought. The psychiatrist decided to give me a prescription for valium, a drug to calm my nerves. I believe he thought that was all I wanted. I refused to take the prescription. I told the doctor that I could get those on the street all day.

I went back to the VA and was able to convince the director (by lying) that I had a drug problem. You see, I learned that the VA had a drug rehab program for veterans. The director decided that I could be in the program for thirty days. What's a mystery to me is that the VA wanted to prescribe drugs for me but did not want to admit me to the program unless I was having a drug dependency.

Like I learned while in the Marine Corps, you must be determined with a laser focus on what you want or need! Never take "no" from a person that cannot tell you "yes," if what you want is reasonable.

In the fall of 1971, I started what was a program to help veterans rehabilitate from using drugs. There were daily group and individual counseling meetings with the veterans. I enjoyed the individual counseling; it empowered me greatly. I still did not have a plan for myself once the thirty days were over.

I would call my mother periodically to assure her that I was doing fine. I told her that I was in California with my cousin, Leo, who I reconnected with as a teenager and again in the Marine Corps. Leo did go to Vietnam, was wounded, and received a Purple Heart. Once he was released, he married and moved from Baltimore to California.

A Phone Call That Redirected My Life

ON ONE SUCH PHONE CALL, my mother mentioned that a neighbor named Frances was asking about me. Frances lived in my family's neighborhood. I would see her at the bus stop on my way to college. I carried a briefcase to look smart.

"Why the briefcase?" Frances asked me one day.

I blushed and told her that I was studying to become an accountant. I did not see or speak with Frances again until many months later. One day, Frances asked my mother whether I was still in college or if I had completed my studies. She wanted my mother to have me call her soon.

It was good that I called my mother and unexpectedly discovered that Frances had asked about me. I called Frances to ask why she wanted me to contact her. Apparently, Frances worked at City Hall for the mayor of Baltimore. The mayor's human resources director needed someone with some accounting skills.

First, I found it hard to believe that Frances, of all people, worked for the mayor's office, yet it was true. She told me that her office was looking for someone with the accounting skills required for a job that was posted. Frances wanted to see if I would be willing to work on a trial basis at Baltimore City Hall. I visited City Hall, where I worked for two days on an unpaid trial and was hired after the trial with pay and benefits.

Wow, what a turn of events! Especially since I was on Day 25 of the thirty-day VA program. I still had no place to live when I left the hospital, but I had a job.

Yet the blessed timing continued. I still exercised daily. On Day 26, while I was out exercising, I saw Granny! We were both surprised to see one another. Granny was visiting one of her nephews, a veteran at the same hospital. I shared that I was at the hospital getting my life in shape, but I would be leaving soon with no place to live. Before Granny departed, she told me to come see her once I left the hospital.

I told the director of the VA program that I was hired by the mayor's office and would start work in two days. The director informed me that he was extending my stay at the hospital until I received a few paychecks and that the hospital would provide lunch and bus tokens for me. This would allow me to save money to have a place to live! What a blessing!

Pressman Street Living

I MET WITH GRANNY to discuss my living situation. Granny introduced me to Mr. Landlord, whose name I cannot remember. Mr. Landlord did not like young people my age. I was twenty-three years old at the time. His position was that young people were destructive and unruly, so he did not want to rent me one of his apartments. So, after that, as a grown man, I was living with Granny once again, but temporarily, I hoped!

Every day, I would go to work at City Hall, return home, do my outdoor exercises, then remain indoors for the evening. I began to sit on the front porch some evenings as I started to paint by the numbers to occupy my time. Well, the neighbors thought I was an artist because I had an easel, a paintbrush, and photos of what I was painting. I never let on that it was paint by the numbers! After about a month, Mr. Landlord, who, unbeknown to me was observing my behavior, decided that I was a young person that he could trust to take care of his property. He finally rented me one of his apartments.

His building was a triplex, with Granny on the top level and empty apartments on the middle and bottom levels. He decided to rent me the middle apartment for $35 a week, so I accepted the offer. The apartment was located at 3122 Pressman Street. When I entered the building, a small door to my apartment was on the right.

Inside the apartment were a living room, a bedroom, a kitchen area without a stove or other kitchen appliances, and a gorgeous bathroom with a stained glass shower door. I did not need much else. I was used to buying my meals, mostly at sandwich shops. My martial arts class was held in a playground area across from my apartment. This earned me the nickname, "The Karate Man," from the teenagers in the neighborhood.

I was happy without friends because I was feeling God's grace.

I informed the director of the VA program that I had secured a place to live before the extra time that I was granted. I was a success story for the program because I was working and found a place to live before leaving the hospital. Many veterans left on harder times than before they entered the program.

In those two months, my life changed for the better. I went from homeless with no plans to getting a one-time check from the state of Maryland's Social Services department, convincing the powers-to-be to accept me into a rehabilitation program, being blessed with an accounting clerk position at the mayor of Baltimore's office, and being blessed with my own living quarters. Now, I began to understand that my steps were truly ordered by God!

The timing was set in motion from birth to now. Every step I took from Castle Street to Joseph Avenue to the Marine Corps to Bethune Road to my new home on Pressman Street with more that came were ordered steps.

I know what you are thinking. What about the lies you told?

All I can say is that I did repent!

Working at the
Mayor's Office

I WORKED AT THE MAYOR of Baltimore's office Monday through Friday from 8 a.m. until around 5 p.m. During the 1970s, the mayor was William Donald Schaffer. Mr. Schaffer was a city councilman and then president of the City Council before becoming mayor. He probably was re-elected twice as mayor before becoming the Comptroller of Maryland. Later, he was elected Governor of Maryland. What a career he experienced!

My job as a statistician was calculating the percentage of Baltimore City participants in city-funded programs for the elderly and youth. I was in a unit with four women, and we processed the statistical data for the city.

I worked for the mayor's community executive, Mr. Quentin Lawson. I drove Mr. Lawson to his appointments all over the city of Baltimore. Eventually, he began to see potential in me that I was unaware of, and he used these driving trips to mentor me. He told me that I was good enough to be greater in life. He noticed that I was shy because I thought that I was not educated enough to be successful.

With Mr. Lawson's mentoring, I grew to understand that my future was waiting for me to decide on how to achieve my goals. I just had to learn how to set plans and goals for my life and then pursue them without fear of failing.

Riding With Granny

While I worked at the mayor's office, Granny worked at the Baltimore Gas & Electric Company, which was also in downtown Baltimore. Granny drove to work, and some days, when I did not travel by bus, I would ride with her. However, Granny was a two-foot driver. This meant she had her right foot on the gas and her left foot on the brake—at the same time! I have no idea how she coordinated this without confusing the two pedals. She would start to pray as she roared the engine with the gas pedal while the car was in park. Then, she would jerk the gear from Park to Drive as she hit the gas pedal. We would take off as if on an amusement park ride.

One snowy day, she decided that I should drive. In Baltimore, snow sometimes turned into ice, which made driving slippery. Well, that did not faze Granny! She wanted me to hit the gas as if the roads were clear. I was afraid of the car sliding or hitting other vehicles. Granny would pop me on the back of my head if I slowed down and say, "Drive, boy! Don't stop this car. I got to get to work!"

Anyhow, I decided to catch the bus to work.

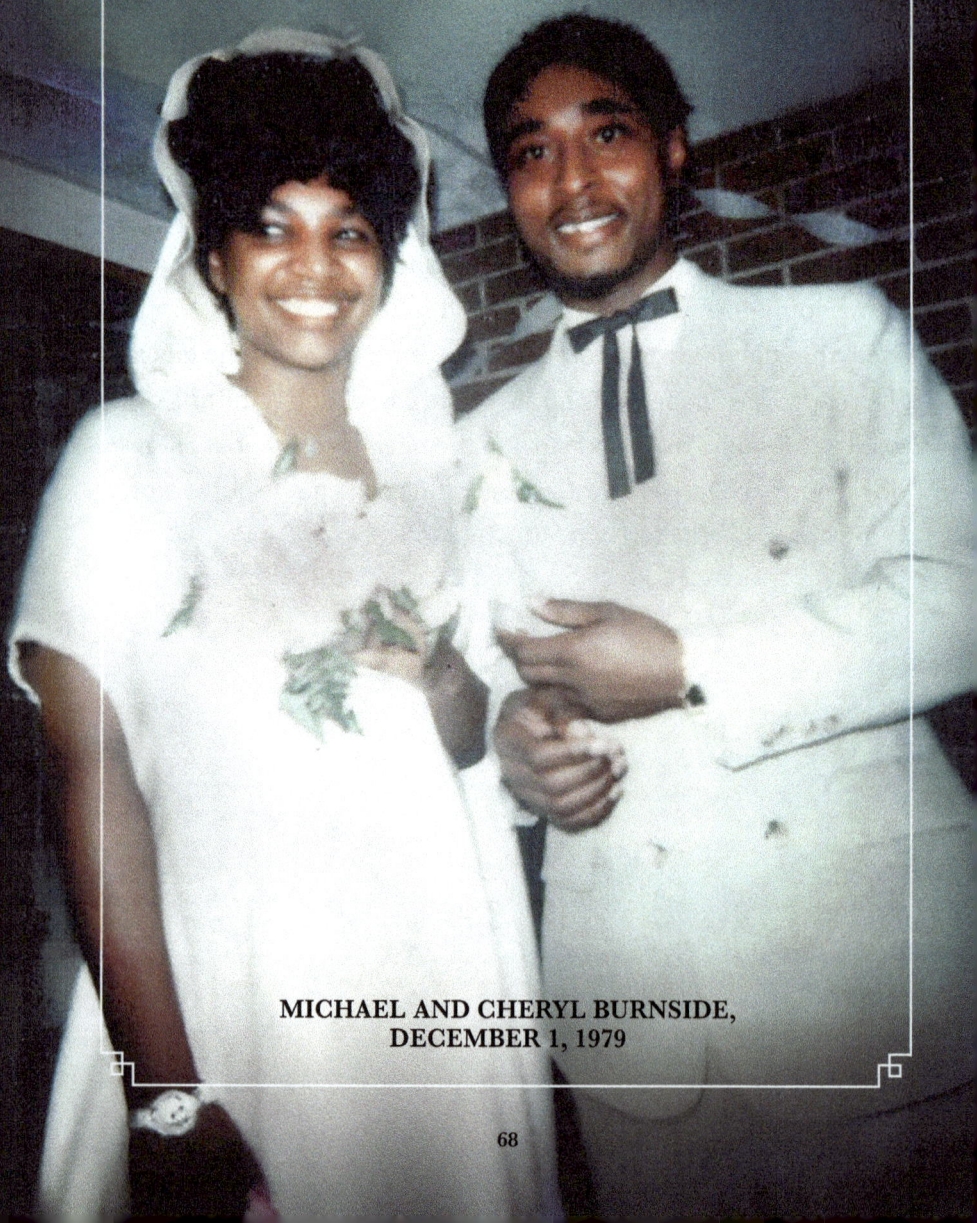

A Love Story

**MICHAEL AND CHERYL BURNSIDE,
DECEMBER 1, 1979**

Finding Cinderella

I AM BLESSED to have a few good friends in my life, and one of my best friends is Cheryl, the lady I married.

Cheryl's first cousin, Patricia, who was my co-worker, first introduced me to Cheryl by inviting me to a jazz club in 1978. Several other co-workers attended the event, but Patricia arranged for me to ride in Cheryl's car to the club. While the music played and people danced, I was a wallflower. I had no emotion. I was not in the mood to dance, date, or be friends with anyone at this time in my life. Since she drove to the club, with a guilty conscience I asked Cheryl to dance to the last song.

It was a year later, to the day, before I saw Cheryl again. In 1979, her cousin Patricia invited me to a fashion show. This time, I was interested enough to get to know her better. I looked at Cheryl in her colorful dress and styled hair, but I did not get a chance to see her shoes.

You see, this is a Cinderella story. I had to get her digits. *(Digits were what we called phone numbers.)*

When the show was over, I wanted to speak with Cheryl, but I lost track of her, and I was extremely disappointed. I left the venue to see if I could find her, but there were no glass slippers. I spoke with Patricia to get her location, hoping to see her again. Cheryl lived more than fifty miles from my city! Since I did not have a vehicle, I could not see how I would be able to visit her.

Afterward, Patricia told me that Cheryl was attending the

University of Maryland, the very hospital where I was born. What a coincidence!

On a rainy day, I decided to type her a letter reintroducing myself and asking if I could visit her at the university. When I think about why I wrote to her, or why I typed her a letter, or even why I wanted to see her again, I have not one answer. But if you sit on a question long enough, an answer will appear.

So, I can now answer that question. I was in love and did not know it yet. You see, God gave me a choice like he gave Solomon, except my choice was whether I wanted to be materially wealthy or whether I wanted everlasting love. I chose love, not just unilateral love, where only one loves the other, but bilateral love, where both parties love each other.

Cheryl invited me to visit her at the university, so I boarded a city bus on a nice warm day to see her. We met and talked awhile until Cheryl popped the unthinkable question.

"Let's go somewhere," she said.

Going somewhere, in my mind, meant driving somewhere, and, of course, I did not have a car! My heart skipped several beats.

Just so you know why, before I met Cheryl, I had the opportunity to go on a date with a lady who worked in the same vicinity where I worked in Baltimore. We arranged to meet at the woman's house to go out to a nightclub. On a nice mellow evening, I knocked on her door. I cannot even remember her name. She was ready for a night of partying. She and I proceeded to walk toward North Avenue, where I was planning to hail a cab. She thought we were walking to get my car.

After a few blocks, she said, "Where is your car?"

"Oh, I do not have a car," I said. "We are walking to North Avenue to hail a taxicab."

That's right, a taxicab, because in 1977, Uber or Lyft was not born yet!

Anyway, she said, "I am sorry, but I do not date men without equipment." *(I am not sure what else comes under the category of equipment besides a car.)*

So, back to the Cinderella story. When Cheryl wanted to go somewhere with me, my not having any equipment scared me! I was afraid to ask, but I did anyway.

"Where do you want to go?"

To my surprise, Cheryl said, "It is such a lovely day. Let's walk to the Baltimore Harbor."

A woman after my own heart! A woman who only wanted to walk! I was falling in love at that moment.

Think of all the ways we meet people, the journey we travel with people through good and tough times. It is a blessing to find a friendship that lasts with no end in sight.

Once I found Cheryl's location, our friendship began. All because a woman did not care that I did not have any equipment.

Since 1979 Cheryl and I have gotten friendlier each year!

One day, very unexpectedly, Cheryl asked me, "Do you want a roommate?"

"Why?" I answered.

"Because I will not have a dorm room, and I would have to commute fifty miles from Belair to Baltimore every day for class," she said.

You can now see how the entrapment started.

"Okay, just for a while," I said.

To my surprise, Cheryl was now basically living with me. This was unexpected!

Then family and even neighbors started being curious about Cheryl and me. One day, while visiting my place, Granny had a

71

conversation with Cheryl about me. I had no idea of what was said, except for Cheryl's version of their chat.

Then, my mother and Aunt Margaree visited my place while I was at work, and Cheryl was in the apartment. Cheryl claims my aunt searched my closets, but she is uncertain of what she was looking for. I believe my mother, Granny, and aunt wanted to know what Cheryl and my plans were.

Next, a lady neighbor stopped me one day on my way home from work to tell me that it was a shame to have all these different women coming to my place every day. I had no idea who these different women were. I eventually found out that it was Cheryl, who liked to change her hairstyle often!

I worked Monday through Friday while Cheryl attended classes when the classes met. I began to get concerned about Cheryl being still in bed when I left for work, so I became paranoid. One day, when I got to work, I called to tell Cheryl to get her things and leave my apartment because I did not want a roommate.

Unbeknownst to me, she thought, "Wow, this is the man for me!"

Two days after Cheryl left, I received a three-to-four-page letter from her sharing her feelings for me. We reunited and the rest is history!

Leaving Pressman Street

WHILE LIVING WITH ME on Pressman Street, Cheryl graduated from the University of Maryland as a physical therapist around 1979. She had already earned a B.S. degree from Hampton University in 1976. She got her first job with a nice salary with Griffin Physical Therapy and decided to get her first apartment. This meant that she would be leaving me on Pressman Street since I had no plans for anything else.

Cheryl started apartment hunting in Baltimore, but she had always wanted to leave Maryland. Me, not so much. In fact, I had no thoughts of leaving Baltimore, let alone the state of Maryland. Cheryl wanted to move to Raleigh, North Carolina.

Cheryl found an apartment in a complex near Reisterstown Mall in Baltimore. She was so happy, her first solo apartment by herself, or so she thought. At first the apartment agent told Cheryl she would need a co-signer. When she shared this news with me, I told her what my granny told me about co-signers.

"You tell those people, that you are a hard-working young lady with a job, and you will be certain to pay your rent on time."

Sure enough, Cheryl told the agent what I said to say, so the agent approved her for an apartment on her own signature!

I was so excited for her until I realized that she would be leaving me. Wow, it just dawned on me that I may lose her! I had thoughts of her meeting someone else and forgetting all about me, so I had a brilliant idea.

"Take me with you," I said.

Somehow, she did, so we moved to 6617 Eberle Drive in a basement apartment in August 1979. We married on December 1, 1979. Yes, you read it correctly. We married about three months after moving in together!

I asked my granny, a spiritual-minded lady, "Granny, is it wrong of someone to live with someone they love before they are married?"

"Would you buy a pair of shoes before trying them on?" Granny said.

"No," I said.

"That is all I got to say about that," Granny replied.

Apparently, Granny was right. As I write this story in 2024, Cheryl and I will celebrate forty-five years of a fantastic marriage. Thank you, Jesus!

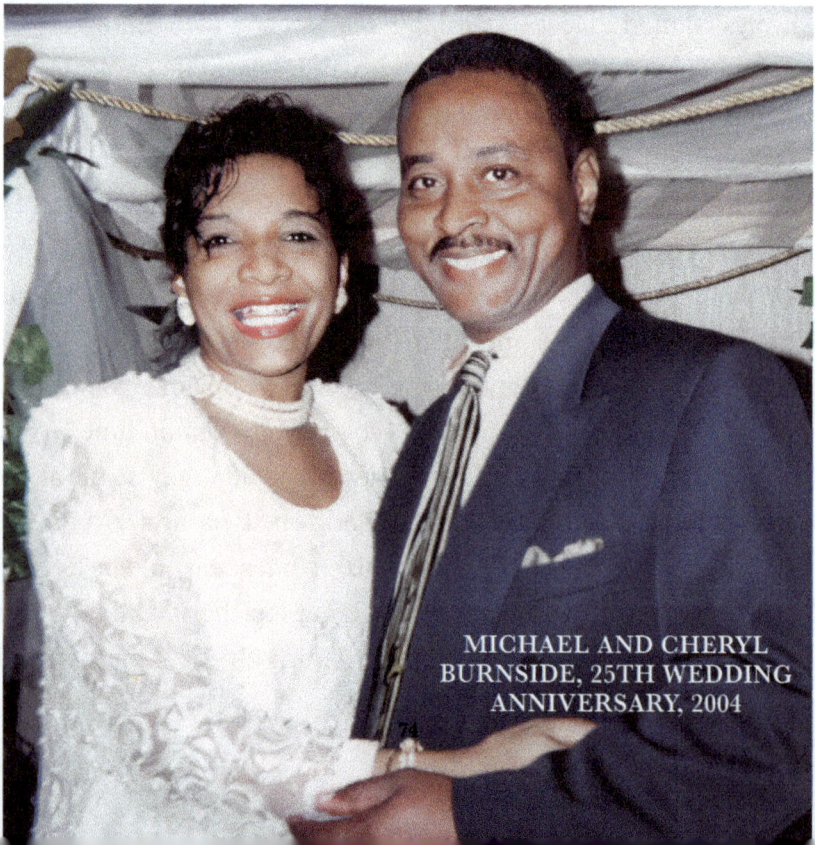

MICHAEL AND CHERYL BURNSIDE, 25TH WEDDING ANNIVERSARY, 2004

The Burnsides

Decision To Move South, But Where?

AFTER WE WERE MARRIED, Cheryl wanted to fulfill her wish to leave Maryland and live in North Carolina. I, on the other hand, did not want to move out of Maryland. What a dilemma!

Then I remembered as a student at Morgan State College in 1977, I attended an event where Nikki Giovanni, the poet, was speaking. Nikki challenged students to visit a city that they had never visited before. I was so excited, that I rushed home to a lonely apartment on Pressman Street after the event.

Once I got home, I wrote the names of five cities on strips of paper and put these in a bowl on the table. I randomly pulled a strip out of the bowl, and it read "Atlanta, Georgia." Wow!

I made plans to take a train from Baltimore to Atlanta the very next week. I calculated that I only had enough money to stay for two nights in a hotel, plus the cost of the train. When I got to Atlanta, I was so excited but had no idea where to go, nor did I know a single person in Georgia.

I decided to take a taxi to downtown Atlanta to get a hotel, perhaps a Holiday Inn. I thought I could afford such a hotel. But on the drive, I began to see the skyline of Atlanta from a distance. I then saw what I had never seen before in my life! A hotel with their elevators on the outside of the building. I was so amazed. So, I asked the taxi driver to take me to that hotel. This was one of the tallest hotels in Atlanta, the Westin Peachtree Plaza. I felt like I was in New York City! I did not know how I was to pay for a room, but I was going to stay there. As I went to register for a room, when I opened my wallet, my student I.D. fell out.

"Oh, are you a student?" the desk clerk asked.

"Yes, I am."

"Well then, your room rate is half off this week," she said.

"Give me four nights," I said.

I was lonely in Atlanta, but I enjoyed what sights I saw.

Moving On Up (Down)
To Atlanta

SO IN 1980, when Cheryl wanted to move to North Carolina and I did not want to leave Maryland, I decided to compromise. Since I had been to Atlanta and I was in love with Cheryl, I said, "Oh, I would like to check out Atlanta."

We first visited Cheryl's Aunt Barbara, her husband, Sherman Sr., and her four cousins in College Park, Georgia, a suburb close to Atlanta. We did not know anyone else. We stayed a couple of days with them and then returned to Baltimore. A few weeks later, more determined to move South, we returned to the Hilton Hotel for a week. The hotel room rate was negotiated by the brother of Cheryl's friend, Valerie, at a discounted rate.

This time we had the chance to look for apartments. On the last day before we returned to Baltimore, we found a suitable apartment that we both liked. Excited, the two of us went back home, packed, and moved to Atlanta without a job for either of us. You are talking about blind faith: we had it!

Our song was Jeffery Osborne's, *We're Going All the Way*.

We drove to Atlanta with one car when we left Baltimore. Our new home was a spacious, first-floor apartment with two bedrooms on Druid Hills Road in Northeast Atlanta. Cheryl was employed by South Fulton Hospital in southwest Atlanta as a physical therapist. I was an unemployed accountant, preparing tax returns when I could find clients. Eventually, I worked temporary accounting assignments with companies.

Cheryl could find work easily as a therapist in other physical therapy clinics. That was great, because she did not stay long if she was not satisfied. Cheryl became a partner with the owner of one of the clinics where she worked. This allowed her to be self-employed for over twelve years. Meanwhile, I was still searching for full-time work, with only temporary assignments, until one of the temp jobs offered me a full-time position with a company car and a decent salary with some catches!

The job was a temporary auditing assignment, but I was not selected for full-time placement at first. I was later called by the owner, who was Congressman John Linder, to teach two individuals he had hired full-time to perform audits. When it became apparent that the employees were not able to perform the audits to Mr. Linder's expectation, I was offered a full-time position. However, I had applied for a teaching position with the Atlanta Public Schools to teach at a technical college. The timing was such that I was also offered the chance to teach accounting at the college. After prayer, I realized that even though Mr. Linder's company paid about $10,000 more with a company car, my future was in education. So I chose the teaching position. It was the right decision. I retired from Atlanta Technical College with a pension in June 2021 after thirty-seven years of service. What a blessing!

Cheryl and I began to enjoy southern living in Georgia. We explored the state's parks, rivers, and mountains. We went to plays and events living up to the Atlanta life. We enjoyed our jobs and made new friends at work. It was a slow process, getting used to the difference in the South. Most of all, we were getting to know each other better. I believe we realized that it was just the two of us.

"We need a child," Cheryl said one day.

"What for?" I asked.

"We have been married for years, and we have nothing to show for it," she replied.

"We cannot have children until we buy a home," I said.

So, we bought a house, and Cheryl said, "Now what?"

Anyway, I cannot remember what happened, other than we eventually ended up with two sons! I am so grateful that she won. I love having those boys!

Cheryl's family visited us a couple of times when we first moved to Atlanta. I know her father, Willard, was very proud of us. Most importantly, both her father and mother were proud of Cheryl. Cheryl was the third oldest child of six siblings, five girls and one boy. She wanted to move from Belair, Maryland, because she was bored with the town. She felt there was more to life than the town where she grew up. She always wanted to move to a college town, like Raleigh, North Carolina.

We were both pleased about our move to Atlanta. Yet, we missed the family, food, and places we left in Maryland. I missed Baltimore and my family, especially since my siblings rarely visited. However, Joseph did visit as often as he could. Of course, I would travel to Baltimore quite a lot until I was no longer homesick!

Now that we were settled with our life in Atlanta, it was not the Cinderella story. Meaning, that once I married Cinderella, it was not "happily ever after." Our Maryland families were having life issues. Both Cheryl and my father were experiencing physical illness. Cheryl's father, Willard, suffered from heart and breathing issues. My father, William, who was a smoker, suffered from lung and breathing issues as well.

My father died in 1987 in Baltimore when Cheryl and I lived in Atlanta. Cheryl's father, Willard, died in 1990, while we were in Maryland visiting family. Both losses were devastating to the families.

MICHAEL AND CHERYL, 1985

Traveling Through
A Snowstorm

MY FATHER, WILLIAM, was experiencing some pain in his lungs and was admitted to the hospital in Baltimore. I took a weekend flight to visit him, but he died before I landed. I was unable to even see him before he died and before I had to leave that weekend.

I had to return to Atlanta to check on Cheryl because we were expecting our first child, Michael II. Cheryl had a miscarriage about a year before this pregnancy because of fibroids in her body. I was supposed to stay with Cheryl because she was having another tough pregnancy. Since I was the oldest sibling of seven, with only five of us surviving at that time, Cheryl strongly suggested that I should drive back to Baltimore to be with my family while she remained in Atlanta. I would not have gone, but she insisted, so I did try to make the journey back to Baltimore. Cheryl felt that I would feel guilty if I did not attend the funeral. I, too, believed that I would regret not attending my dad's homegoing.

I left early Monday morning, on February 23, 1987, for a twelve-hour car ride only to encounter the beginning of a snowstorm once I entered South Carolina. I had the heat and radio blasting in the brown Cutlass I was driving north on Interstate 85. Soon, white snow blanketed the road, making the driving lanes no longer visible. Due to the hazardous visibility conditions, I veered off to the left to avoid a tractor-trailer, only to slide down an embankment into a ditch. I attempted to drive out of the ditch, but the wheels began to spin in place. I got out of the car to see if I could put something under the wheels to help the car move, and when I did, the door closed and locked with the engine running, music playing, and the heat still on. The temperature was about thirty degrees. I did not even have my coat on! My coat was inside the car!

A tow truck appeared after about forty minutes. I flagged the driver down, and he pulled me out of the ditch for $50. I was on my way again to Baltimore! However, I did not get far. I made it only to North Carolina before I slid once again off the road into another ditch. Before getting out of the car this time, I put my coat on, unlocked all the car doors, and turned the radio and heater off. This time it was dark, about nine o'clock in the evening, with limited traffic driving by.

I attempted to flag someone down to help me push my car out of the ditch, but no one stopped. Finally, a small old-style yellow Volkswagen Beetle stopped. Out jumped a skinny young man with no shirt on in thirty-degree weather. The young man asked me if I needed help pushing the car out of the ditch. First, I was just looking at him. Did he think that just the two of us could push this heavy car out of a snow-covered ditch and up a snowy hill back to the road?

The young man assessed the situation and then said, "We are going to need more help."

I thought, without saying, "I could have told you that, but where are we going to get any help with no one in sight?"

Undeterred, the young man went up the hill and, within a couple of minutes, flagged down three vehicles. Several men got out and helped push my car back on the road!

This was Monday night, and the funeral was Tuesday, so I knew I could make it by Tuesday morning, even if I were traveling at a slow speed. After less than an hour, North Carolina State Police stopped me. The police were asking everyone to get off the roads because it was too dangerous to travel. Police asked me where I was headed.

Once I told them that I was headed to Baltimore, they told me to find a hotel for the night and head back to Atlanta in the morning. Hotels in the area were booked, but I was able to find a room after I traveled about five miles.

Okay, I would just wait until Tuesday morning, and even if I missed the funeral, I would be there with the family Tuesday afternoon. Tuesday morning, I woke up to cars, including mine, covered with snow. The hotel clerk let me use a broom to brush the snow from the car. The state police would not allow me to travel north to Baltimore. I called my family, but they knew about the storm since it was broadcast on the news.

With so many obstacles in my path, I decided to head back to Atlanta. Unfortunately, I missed my father's funeral and being with my family, but fortunately, I returned in time to get Cheryl to the hospital since she was alone. You see, Cheryl's difficult pregnancy was with a disease called toxemia, which could have taken her life. My understanding is that toxemia dumps poison in a pregnant woman's body. Therefore, the baby should be born immediately to prevent her from being poisoned. When I walked into the bedroom, I knew she had to go to the hospital immediately. The doctors had to induce labor for the baby, who was born prematurely.

On Tuesday, February 24, 1987, as my father was being buried, my first son, Michael II, was born. He weighed six pounds, six ounces. Yes, this was such a great journey, but the hardest part was losing my father during this same time. Life does give and take, but this journey was a miracle.

Then Came
Michael Perry Burnside 2nd

CHERYL AND I WERE PROUD to have a healthy son. I named Michael the "2nd" because I did not want a son called Junior. I was thirty-six and Cheryl was thirty-three years of age. We were delighted to be parents finally. I took Michael outside and held him up toward the sky and dedicated him to God!

Michael was a shy child and very private as he was growing up. Once Cheryl returned to work, he was in several daycare centers. I was so overprotective of Michael that if I did not like how he was treated, I would not return him to that center the next day. He learned easily and was very good academically in school. He started reading at three years old. We never had to assist him with his homework assignments or even provide a tutor.

Michael attended a Christian academy called Solid Rock until he was five years old. He then started first grade at a private Montessori school called Counterpane. We thought this school would broaden his education, but we later learned that Michael did not like Counterpane, so we enrolled him in Fayette County public schools, starting with second grade. He remained enrolled in Fayette County schools until he graduated.

Michael worked various jobs while in high school. He worked for the Coca-Cola company stacking drink products in grocery stores. He also worked as a waiter in a small restaurant close to home. In his senior year of high school, Michael mentored Hispanic children in a nearby elementary school.

When he graduated from high school, Cheryl and I bought him a blue Volvo from Cheryl's Uncle Napoleon, who lived in Hampton, Virginia. Uncle Napoleon brought the car to the United States from Germany. Michael was so overjoyed to have his very own car!

Michael attended Georgia Southern University after high school. Georgia Southern was located in Statesboro, Georgia, two hundred miles from our home. Michael's grades earned him a Georgia Hope Scholarship that paid for his tuition for all four years of college. Like his dad, Michael majored in accounting and finance but claimed he did not like accounting. Michael was a great A and B student as far as his grades were concerned, and he pledged to a fraternity while in college.

During college, he met Shalonda, whom he became fast friends with. *(More on Shalonda later.)* I did not want my sons to date while they were in high school because I wanted them to focus on getting their priorities in order.

Michael II Becomes
An Adult

MICHAEL GRADUATED FROM COLLEGE in May 2009 with a degree in accounting and returned home unsure of what he wanted to do with his life. He started working for a company owned by a friend of our family. It took a while for Michael to focus on what he wanted to do about work. Cheryl was not happy with him for not using his education as an accountant for employment.

Around 2011, Michael took a position in the hills of Western North Carolina as a camp counselor for a summer camp. While he was working at the camp, his Volvo died and he had no transportation. Around this time, my mother, Michael's grandmother, decided that she did not want to drive her car anymore and wanted to give her car to her grandson. Wow! The timing was great and Michael wanted out of the hills of North Carolina, so he found a way to travel to Baltimore to receive the car from his grandmother.

You see, Michael was secretly in love with Shalonda, who was now living in North Carolina. Now with a car, Michael could visit her. So, Michael decided to enroll at A&T State University, just to be near Shalonda, I suspect. He was studying finance, supposedly, but I think he was really studying Shalonda. I assume the timing was off because Shalonda was not thinking that he was the one yet!

So, in 2012, at 25 years of age, Michael returned home to Cheryl and me, his beloved parents, without a job. We were concerned about his future. He did not have a plan that we were aware of. However,

Cheryl and I were very pleased that Michael was no longer in the mountains at that campsite. The fact is, we disliked him being alone in the mountains with no way out.

After a while, his mother wanted him to start his career and move out of our house! I, on the other hand, knew what he was up against as a young man just getting started. I, too, wanted him to get a career job, especially before he started a family, but I was not so concerned about him moving out of the house at that time.

Since he was not working and was perhaps slow at finding meaningful employment, his mother became an employment agency. This meant that Cheryl was finding hook-ups for Michael to become employed. She asked people in her network about job opportunities for her son. There were people she knew in Coca-Cola Company. She even asked her physical therapist partner to interview Michael.

That was a disaster, because the partner did not want to hire Michael and Michael did not want to be hired. Finally, an associate of Cheryl's connected Michael with an accounting position at her company. Now Michael was off and established with a great job and benefits!

Remember Shalonda? Shalonda graduated from college with a marketing degree. I am not sure about the details of her move to Atlanta. Now that both were working, they decided to visit Denver. Why? I am not sure, except that we did find out that a proposal to marry was made and accepted. So, in April 2015, they were married in Georgia. Such a wonderful wedding!

Then one weekend, Michael and Shalonda met with Cheryl and me at a Macy's in Atlanta to tell us that they were moving to Denver, Colorado. Of course, we were happy and excited for them. You see Cheryl and I left Baltimore, Maryland, to live in Atlanta, Georgia. We knew that it is great to uproot and start fresh in a new town!

MICHAEL II AND SHALONDA

Girls Added to
The Burnsides

MICHAEL AND SHALONDA'S move to Denver proved fruitful. When Michael married Shalonda, we added the first female besides Cheryl to the Burnside family. Shalonda was to us the daughter that we never had. Yes, this took some getting used to, but it did not take long before we began to love her and her family as well.

One day, we received a video of Michael and Shalonda doing a baby dance. It took a moment for us to understand that they were telling us they were expecting a baby. What a joyful moment that was! Later, in 2017, a baby girl was born, adding to the Burnside family. Three years later, in 2020, another baby girl appeared, increasing the Burnside females by three to make four with Grandmother Cheryl!

At some point Michael and Shalonda decided to move to Texas to start life with their new family. Both girls and Shalonda's birthdays are in November—how exciting! In April of 2024, Michael and Shalonda celebrated their ninth wedding anniversary. They started a gourmet popcorn business in honor of their daughters.

MICHAEL II AND SHALONDA

WADE BURNSIDE, 2011

What About
Brother Wade

MY SECOND SON, Wade Arthur, was born, and we knew that he was a blessing. His mother spent almost five months on bed rest, at least four of those months were spent in Piedmont Hospital in Atlanta, followed by a month at home. We did not know what to expect with his birth. The medical team decided that he would be born a month before his due date. In fact, Wade was born after seven months of pregnancy. The little fellow was only a little over four pounds. He did not do the expected cry. I told the doctors not to spank him either. (I never liked beating children.) Wade eventually cried out. I did not realize doctors like to hear an outcry to ensure the baby's lungs are okay.

Cheryl was very weak after Wade's delivery. Once she was released from the hospital, to her dismay, she went home without baby Wade. You see, at that time the hospital thought it was in the best interest of the newborn to weigh over five pounds before the child was released from the hospital's care.

However, baby Wade would not take his formula from the nurses and was losing ounces of weight. Therefore, I would leave work each day to arrive at the hospital during feeding time to make sure he was fed. Fortunately, he did allow me to feed him. Meanwhile, Cheryl was at home concerned that she could not be with her baby. I would leave Wade to go back to work, leave work, then come home to my sad wife. I do not even remember how long this struggle went on. I just remember talking with Cheryl about when the hospital would release her boy.

Since Wade still had not reached their five-pound requirement, I decided to ask whether it was illegal to take my son home to be with his parents.

"No," was the answer, it was just their opinion that it was in the best interest of the child to remain in the hospital. Well, Cheryl and I thought it was in the best interest of the family that we bring Wade home.

The hospital had no choice but to release our son to his parents. This decision was best for the hospital, the parents, and baby Wade. Once home, it did not take Wade long before he was well over five pounds. Love is all it takes sometimes!

As a growing child, Wade was always in a rush or in a hurry going nowhere. He was very fast in his movements; we called him Speedo. Wade's speed caused him to crash into walls when he attempted to cut corners. His speeding caused great anxiety with his chores and schooling. He just did not want to take time to do anything that required more than a quick fix! So, he struggled in school with completing assignments.

Wade was first enrolled in a Montessori school for eleven months, then Grace Christian Academy for preschool, then East Fayette Elementary School for kindergarten and first grade, then Fayette Intermediate School. Then he was transferred to Fayette Middle School, then to Flat Rock Middle School, and finally to Sandy Creek High School. He attended a few schools, to say the least!

Wade struggled in high school until the eleventh grade, but he finally improved enough to be accepted to Georgia Southern University, the same school his brother attended. Wade was so excited when we brought him to the campus for the first time.

Michael had graduated from that same university two years before Wade began.

Wade's first reaction to seeing so many young women was that he lost his composure or his mind! I explained to him that his goal was to complete his degree in four years. He was not to change majors. He was to graduate or quituate–a word that I made up–in those four years.

Wade's major was business and marketing, but his heart was music. He wanted to become a music producer. You see, since he was around twelve years old, that is what he dreamed of. He felt that we forced him to go to college and major in what we wanted. Parents, be careful not to plan your children's lives based on your expectations.

Wade did complete four years of college. To date, however, he does not have enough credits to complete his degree and graduate.

Before returning home, Wade accepted internships with "In Love With Music," "Music is My Business," "Black Celebrity Giving," "Defiant Management," "Grand Hussle Records," "Winners Circle Publishing," and "BoB Label." He was not always paid, but he believed in his ability, as did his mother and I. Now, in 2024, Wade has moved to Atlanta and purchased his own transportation after tearing my car apart. He has a fantastic lady friend who keeps him on target for a greater life.

Wade is working with a host of talented up-and-coming artists in the music industry. He has helped his clients produce music as well as helping them get paid. Wade has also written a couple of books, Producers Only, and How to Get Paid for Your Music! He has clients from other countries with international appeal.

RECORDING ACADEMY CLASS OF 2024 🏆
#IAmTheAcademy

WADE BURNSIDE, 2024

Employment Over
The Years

I WORKED at four and five years old just to earn my birthday and Christmas gifts from my grandparents. You see, my grandparents taught me that in life, you work for what you want. So, I had to announce what home chore I would perform to earn the gifts they provided. However, I did not realize the lesson that I was taught about working to earn what I wanted until later in life.

At age twelve, I made a wood wagon to carry groceries from the supermarket for people at their homes, since many people did not have their own transportation. The hardest part was finding the right wheels that worked on the home-made wagon. Eventually, I used shopping cart wheels.

At fourteen, I told an employer that I was sixteen in order to get a job delivering supermarket advertisements to people's residences. I was the youngest employee, with older men who felt responsible for my well-being. The company would drop crews off in neighborhoods to deliver the advertising flyers to people's homes.

Most people thought of these advertisement papers as trash and did not appreciate them in their homes. People would allow their dogs to chase us away from their gates or doors. We worked in sunshine, cloudy, not too cold, or very light rainy days, but never in harsh weather.

I had a summer job as a file clerk in 1967 at the Social Security Administration in Baltimore, Maryland, when I was sixteen years

Burnside Named Director Of College Placement

Atlanta, Georgia—Atlanta Technical College has announced that Michael Burnside has been promoted to the position of director of college placement.

Reporting directly to Sandra Bryant, vice president of Student Affairs for Atlanta Technical College, Burnside will develop and maintain relationships with employers for the purposes of externship and job placement of enrolled students and graduates. Under his direction, the Career Services Department will meet with students to determine job interests and complete required graduation paperwork, develop job orders from employers, assist in scheduling interviews, and follow up with employers and graduates.

Atlanta Technical College offers employers a 100 percent guarantee that offers to retrain, free-of-charge, any Atlanta Technical College graduate that an employer finds lacking in core competencies. Burnside and his team will maintain the employer satisfaction database and manage the Guarantee Program. Burnside has a 25 year history in higher education and has worked in the

Michael Burnside

Career Services field for more than ten. He was instrumental in helping the college achieve a gross placement rate of 95 percent for the 2010 Atlanta Technical College graduating class.

Atlanta Technical College, a unit of the Technical College System of Georgia, is located in the city of Atlanta, and is an accredited institution of higher education, which provides affordable lifelong learning opportunities, associate degrees, diplomas, technical certificates of credit, customized business and industry training, continuing education, and other learning services, using state-of-the-art technology in more than 100 fields. The integration of academics and applied career preparation to enhance student learning is essential in meeting the workforce demands and economic development needs of the people, businesses, and communities of Fulton County. The college has recently been recognized by *Washington Monthly* magazine as the only Georgia technical college in the top 50 of America's Best Community Colleges and was one of three finalists for the Governor Sonny Perdue Award for the Technical College of the Year.

old. This was an opportunity presented by a social worker visiting our Cherry Hill neighborhood. When I was seventeen, I worked at a fast-food establishment in a mall after high school and on weekends. I was a fry-and-burger boy, then was promoted to cashier before I departed. I enjoyed this job.

Later, I worked as a porter at a hospital in Cherry Hill. Do not let the title fool you! I swept, mopped, and buffed hospital floors. I was proud once I mastered the buffer. I would put a mirror shine on the floors that impressed the supervisors.

In the mid-1970s, I worked as an accounting clerk for both the City of Baltimore and the State of Maryland. Before I left Baltimore to live in Atlanta, I worked at the Maryland National Bank as an auditor, auditing bank clients' financial records. Once in Georgia, in 1983, I worked temporary accounting jobs for corporations in

Atlanta. Since 1982, I have also been self-employed, providing accounting services, including tax preparations.

Finally, in 1984, I secured employment with Atlanta Public Schools as an accounting instructor. I taught accounting to students at Atlanta Technical College for five years . In 1989, I became the Vice-President of Administrative Services. Then, in 1991, I served as business manager for the college.

Later, I had the privilege of serving as an admissions officer and a director of testing before finally becoming the Director of Career Services and a career coach for students. Career coaching was a fantastic job. I hosted career fairs and worked with employers to connect students to jobs.

I enjoyed my work at the college, which sent me to Germany four times on an exchange program to learn about the educational system and the lifestyle of the Germans.

The college sent me to Africa to do college testing for Nigerians. These Nigerians were young men in their twenties who were rebels warring against oil companies. The President of Nigeria, Goodluck Jonathan arranged to have the young men put in camps. The men were paid to receive skilled training in parts of Africa.

The Nigerians decided to have some of the men come to America for training in automotive, computer repair, electrical and heating and air systems. The testing did not go as well as expected, nor did the arrangements to bring the men to America, yet I was able to experience Africa, at least some of the country of Nigeria.

Most of my life's work has been as an accountant. I did not know what I wanted to do in my career early in life. My father and brothers loved working on anything mechanical, especially cars. I did not like getting my hands dirty, so I did not participate in such activities. When I was fifteen, my father said to me that I would have to get a college education in order to earn a living since I refused to work with my hands.

When I decided to attend college, I did not know what major to select, yet I needed a skill. Then I remembered when I was fifteen years old, not understanding why my family owed taxes.

"Who were the people that studied tax laws?" I asked my college counselor.

"They are accountants," the counselor replied.

"That is what I want to do," I said. "I want to become an accountant."

It was a defining moment for me. I wanted to know why my parents owed taxes. You see, people have defining moments but may not realize that moment is leading them in a direction they should go or even alerting them to what their life's purpose is!

MICHAEL BURNSIDE IN THE HANGAR OF THE AVIATION DEPARTMENT AT ATLANTA TECHNICAL COLLEGE, 2008

MICHAEL BURNSIDE AND
JOSEPH (SWEET PEA) JOHNSON, 2021

Family & Friends

Sibling Bookends

IN APRIL 1970, while I was serving in the Marine Corps, the last of the Johnsons was born, Joseph (Sweet Pea) Johnson. The fifth brother and seventh sibling, Joey, was a joy for everyone, even outside of the family, since he was an unexpected but welcome delight.

When I first saw Joseph, he was crawling around on the floor in this baby gown. I thought of the cartoon character Popeye's baby boy. Yes, "Sweet Pea." So, I started calling him Sweet Pea, not knowing that this would become his nickname throughout high school. Cheryl and I thought of him as our son. Sweet Pea's name was so popular that while in high school, Joseph was thought to be absent from class. Even his teacher thought of him as Sweet Pea, not Joseph!

Of the seven children in my family, the two of us became closer over time. I, as the oldest, and Joseph, as the youngest, became friends as well as siblings.

There is a nineteen-year age difference between us. When I was discharged from the Marine Corps in November 1970, Joseph was seven months old. Of course, he was more like a son than a brother at that time. When I married Cheryl, Joseph was nine years old, so Cheryl and I enjoyed taking Joseph to events with us.

Watching Joseph grow up was a pleasure, especially since neither Cheryl nor I had any children then. He graduated from Carver High School in Baltimore, Maryland, in 1988. Joseph was always interested in computers and Information Technology (IT). He is a natural at anything electrical or computer-based.

Joseph worked for the state of Maryland doing emission inspections on vehicles. Then, at some point, he became a Correctional Officer for the state of Maryland. Joseph also started a computer service business to troubleshoot individual and company computer systems. He worked for a few years as a computer guru with a company in the Maryland area, troubleshooting software and hardware issues.

When our mother started having health issues, Joseph stepped up as the youngest to be the caretaker for our mother. This was difficult because Momma thought that her favorite son wanted to do her harm. Yet this did not deter Joseph from caring for our mother with love. He later took our only surviving sister, Rosa, to his home to provide a home for her as well.

I am so grateful and proud of Joseph.

ARTHUR BURNSIDE JR. AND LUTHER JOHNSON

Then There Was Luther

THEN THERE WAS Uncle Luther Johnson, no relationship to William Johnson, but Luther was the brother of Arthur Burnside. It was ironic that Luther had the same last name as the man who became my stepfather, yet was the brother of my biological father!

Around 1982, I met Uncle Luther the same way I met Arthur at seventeen years old. My Aunt Margaree gave me their addresses. I was married to Cheryl when I discovered that Arthur had only one brother. He was fifty-three years old and lived a few miles from where Cheryl and I lived. I contacted Uncle Luther and his wife, Mary, at that time. We arranged a meeting at his house.

I felt his kinship from the moment we met. Uncle Luther attended my graduation from the University of Baltimore. I kept in communication with him while I lived in Baltimore and even when Cheryl and I moved to Georgia in 1983. We are still in touch.

When I visited Baltimore, I would stay with Uncle Luther in his home. He would cook breakfast, and even took me to different restaurants for dinners. Uncle Luther was born in 1928. Still today, in 2024, at the age of 96, he drives his own car, still cooks and takes care of himself, and walks up and down the stairs in his three-story house. He is an inspiration to me and the younger generation.

Uncle Luther was a postal worker for over 30 years. He delivered mail in Baltimore walking door-to-door for as long as it took each day. Later, when he retired from the US Postal Service, he began selling residential real estate. His second wife, Mary Johnson, was a Johnson before they married. Unfortunately, Aunt Mary died when Uncle Luther was in his eighties. Mary was in her seventies when she died. Uncle Luther met his next lady friend, Cassandra, at the age of eighty-eight while she was only seventy years old–seventeen years his junior. In 2024, they have been dating for more than eight years.

UNCLE LUTHER AND MOMMA, 1996

MICHAEL (RIGHT) WITH RONALD JOHNSON, 1970

WILLIAM JOHNSON 2ND

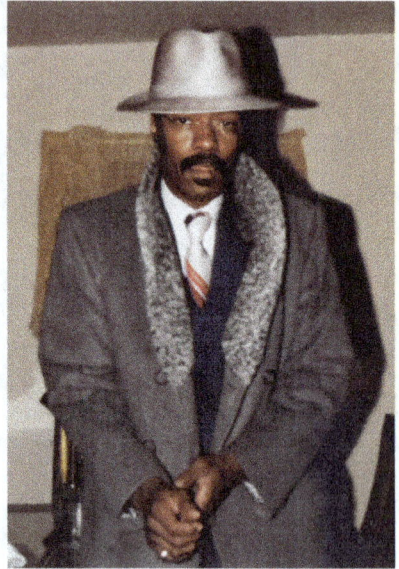

MICHAEL'S COUSIN,
LEO FICKLING JR.

THE JOHNSONS – (FRONT, FROM LEFT) ROSA,
MOMMA DOROTHY, STEVEN; (BACK, FROM LEFT) RONALD,
WILLIAM III, JOEY (SWEET PEA), AND MICHAEL

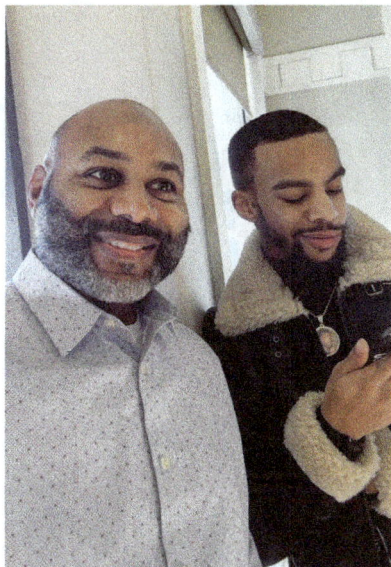

JOSEPH AND HIS SON,
JULIAN JOHNSON

MICHAEL'S SISTER,
BEVERLY JOHNSON

MOMMA'S FAMILY – (FRONT, FROM LEFT) AUNT MARGAREE,
GRANNY, MOMMA DOROTHY; (BACK, FROM LEFT) RONALD
JOHNSON, MICHAEL BURNSIDE, JOEY (SWEET PEA), KRIS
FICKLING (BEHIND MOMMA), WILLIAM JOHNSON III (2000)

Friends and Friendships

friend or friendship – *a state of enduring
affection, esteem, intimacy, and trust between people*

I WANTED TO START with the definition of a friend relationship.
I have not had many friends in my lifetime. I have had associates,
co-workers, and family, but friends are few.

I worked with co-workers for years and thought some of them
were my friends. Yet once I left those jobs, we seldom stayed in
contact with each other. I began to realize that knowing about
people does not make them friends. My father once told me that,
ultimately, you will be able to count true friends on one hand. Real
friends are people who walk in your life when the going gets rough
while others are walking out.

I think about levels of trust with people. It is difficult to understand or know what a person's motives are to become your friend.
Friendships can develop between people but are not always guar-
anteed for life. Friends can be in your life for a short period or for
years with no explanation of why.

Cheryl and I have had meaningful friendships for over twenty years
with Michael and Tammy Lapread, Ed and Stephanie Lawrence,
and Harris and Leah McFerren. These couples were our friends
before our children were born, and we watched them grow from
birth as we did theirs.

Sometimes friendships are developed because of what people
have in common, or perhaps because opposites can attract! Some
friendships did develop from job relationships, such as Freddie

and Ann Hightower and the Rat Pack (Asbury Wilkerson, James Harris, Ronald Laws, Henry Wise, Bobby Sutton, and Damon Scott). I do believe family can have a different kind of relationship than friends, but family can be friends as well. Family friendships with my in-laws grew over time, and they were with Wala, Suad, Terrence, Tammy, and Lisa.

Unfortunately, I cannot list every friend or relationship by name since I must complete my story. Secondly, I do not want to be sued for writing any words that will be untrue! Forgive me if I failed to mention you by name.

A few of my friendships started with conversations about beliefs or desires for living. I do not recall aiming to be friends with anyone because of their status in life or who they were in society. Rather, a genuine liking of the person led me to make friends. Also, different stages and timing in life impacted who I became friends with. Parents must be parents, not friends, with their children to raise them with authority.

MOMMA DOROTHY JOHNSON, 1998

Faith, Forgiveness, & Fragility

A Spiritual Journey
With Beulah Baptist

I WAS INTRODUCED to Jesus from birth. Granny believed in keeping Leo and me in church. From birth to age six, we attended weekly. When I started living with my parents at six years old, church was mentioned but not pursued as much.

When I spent some summers with Rosa Benn, my eighty-three-year-old great-grandmother, we attended church four times a week. Rosa, my mother's grandmother, lived in the projects in West Baltimore. I visited Great-grandmother Rosa more in the summer months than when school was in session. I also visited on some weekends or holidays.

Rosa Benn believed in multi-day visits to church services. I mean Tuesday, Thursday, Friday, and Sunday. Weekdays were Bible study for adults while children listened unattentively. Sundays were all day: eight o'clock a.m. for Sunday school for children, then ten o'clock a.m. for Sunday morning service, then maybe a break before the one o'clock p.m. service and again at four p.m. I began to understand how to use scriptures to live by.

I learned to apply the Bible characters' stories to my life events eventually. I was taught that the acronym for BIBLE was Book of Instructions Before Leaving Earth. This meant I was to learn how to live according to scripture, but this contradicted the environment I was living in.

The church that Great-grandmom attended was a small Baptist

church with services held in the basement of a house in a residential neighborhood on McCulloh Street in West Baltimore. Minister Bishop Bunch was a Bethlehem steelworker without a college education. I later learned that his interpretation of scripture was far from what was intended to inspire saints. His sermons were whooping and hollering about hell and damnation.

I would have been frightened by his sermons about going to hell if I did not feel that I was already in a living hell. Nothing could be any worse than my life was at that time, I thought. You see, even as a child, I felt that God sent Jesus to give me life with more abundance! I did not need to hear what to do, not to go to hell, but rather what to do to survive my miserable existence. Getting to heaven could wait! Sometimes, I believe you can be so heavenly-minded that you are no earthly good.

Yet, I gained a very valuable belief in God, even with an uneducated minister. I was taught about faith, which I base my life on today. The word "faith" can mean what your religious beliefs are, or "faith" is like what Einstein said about imagination: "Imagination is everything. It is the preview of coming attractions."

The whole idea is that if you can imagine what you desire, it may materialize. I have experienced this type of belief in my life. Sometimes when you believe in simple things that you do not even have the power to make happen, your belief in God without a doubt can make it come to pass. This is called faith.

My Thoughts
On Forgiveness

AS A TEENAGER growing up in an urban neighborhood in the 1950s, I thought that there was no hope for me to live the life I dreamed of. I would walk down railroad tracks, wondering if I should hop on a train to get away from the dreary existence that I lived. I would sit by the Chesapeake Bay and look over to the other side, where I could see bright lights. I would dream on a cloudy day that once I got to the other side, the sun would be shining, and all my dreams would be realized.

I felt that my parents had failed me. It had to be their fault that I was not having the exciting life that I was entitled to. At fifteen years old, as I washed dishes, I thought that I was made for more than a domesticated life. As the oldest, I was responsible for washing dishes, cleaning the kitchen, and sweeping and scrubbing floors.

"I did not ask to be born," I told my mother in an argument.

"And I did not ask to bring you here either," she responded.

Not understanding why, what I said to my mother was wrong. Later, I regretted those words.

Looking back, I was angry and unforgiving for years. The real problem was that I did not know that I was unforgiving. I thought I had every right to be angry. Letting go of my unforgiveness was difficult because it was not my fault I was born into the harshness of life. It must be my parents' fault, right? So, I blamed them! You see, unforgiveness is a blindness that prevents you from progressing. Unforgiveness keeps you in the past and prevents you from seeing the future.

Once I realized that I was wrong, I first forgave myself for being wrong, but I did not have to forgive my parents. After all, it was never my parents' fault. This taught me that unforgiveness was like holding my breath. If I did not let it go, it would prevent me from breathing. This leads me to why you must forgive because whenever you bring up past hurts, it only brings the pain back to life. Forgiveness is hard and takes practice. You see, practice makes better, not perfect!

Momma's Changing

I REALIZED THINGS were changing when I watched my mother transition for over two years with dementia before she died at the age of 84 in October 2018. With tears in my eyes, I saw Momma move about in pain. I disliked seeing my mother in pain and I also hated to lose her to death. Then, the Spirit revealed to me that I was not making that decision. For some reason, I realized that the weight I felt was because I thought I had to decide for Momma, yet, that was above my pay grade.

All the years that I would come to Baltimore to visit my mother, I did not suspect that she was experiencing mental changes. In hindsight, I just thought some of her thinking had to do with her getting older. We must be more observant. You see, it is not what you expect, but rather what you inspect. I remember Momma talking about her childhood a lot more, but in negative ways that were unbelievable.

For example, she shared that when she was three years old, in 1937, she traveled one hundred fifty-seven miles from Baltimore, Maryland, to Atlantic City, New Jersey, on a Greyhound bus by herself, and that no adult noticed her missing. Somehow, someone in Atlantic City noticed that a three-year-old girl was alone and boarded her on a return trip by Greyhound bus back to Baltimore. Supposedly, when she returned home, none of the adults, including her parents, had missed her for the entire time she was gone.

The next clue was how paranoid Momma started getting, accusing relatives of stealing from her, even items that she did not possess! Yet, this was not enough for any of the family to think it was dementia. I guess you hope beyond hope that your mother was not suffering from this horrible disease. Life can turn quickly and change what you are used to. Or is it just so hard to accept in the beginning? The song, Everything Must Change, gave me the answer.

Momma had a full life of eighty-four years. She had seven grown children, including me, eleven grandchildren, and even some great-grandchildren. Therefore, Momma had a great life, and her genes were passed on to several generations.

During these difficulties, I did have family and a few friends with me. Life is supposed to be abundant with joy and peace. As I always say, if you cannot change the way it is, then change the way you look at it.

When asked if the glass is half empty or half full, what would you say? I say it depends on what is in the glass.

COVID-19 Pandemic
And Shut-Down

AS I WRITE this part of my story, it is the 21st century, the year 2022, after a horrific pandemic. If we looked at any decade, we would see there have been economic depressions, wars, famine, diseases, discrimination, epidemics–and yet people survived. The pandemic was caused by the worldwide spread of the Covid-19 virus. Nations around the globe went into panic mode and disbelief. How could the world continue to grow and prosper if everything had to shut down? Businesses, colleges, schools, religious organizations, and even some medical facilities closed their doors for an indefinite amount of time. World leaders and health organizations were in mass confusion about how to protect life and the economy.

The saving grace was that the shut-down of face-to-face meetings to engage in business and education came at a time when technology could "Zoom" us together. Yes, people got sick. Some died from this terrible virus. Two of my brothers, Ronald and William III, contracted Covid-19. Ronald died at sixty-six years of age from Covid and other diseases. William III recovered but still, to date, has issues with his lungs because of COVID-19. It is said that nothing lasts forever. That means not only the great times but the unwanted times as well.

News about COVID-19 started airing in late 2019, but it was hard to believe that this virus would cause a shutdown. Once world leaders began to realize that people were getting sick and dying, a strategy had to be developed. Therefore, in March 2020, the United States demanded a shutdown of all social gatherings.

When the pandemic shutdown occurred, I was employed as a career coach for a technical college. My job, in part, was to assist individuals with career choices. This involved providing in-person workshops to help students. I also assisted students as they graduated to gain employment. This involved working with employers, visiting businesses, and setting up interviews with students, graduates, and employers.

Now that a mandatory policy with no social gathering was in place, I was no longer able to have in-person workshops or in-person interviews. I could no longer meet with co-workers and my team in person. This is where technology came to the rescue. To connect with people and to continue work, we used the internet. Issues did arise, of course, with those who did not have internet accessibility or computers. Covid-19 also affected family reunions, and visitations to nursing homes and hospitals. Everyone was even afraid of visiting loved ones or friends because you did not want to be exposed or to give a loved one the virus. The notion that this invisible disease separated all of us from each other caused a great deal of anxiety in everyone.

Then came the conspiracy theories about the vaccine, about how the shots could cause harm. Just like in politics and religion, the theories only created more fear in some and caused a division in others. Our families began to have family Zoom meetings since we live in different cities. We could have been doing this kind of connecting before the pandemic but we just never thought about meeting this way.

MICHAEL BURNSIDE'S GRANDPARENTS,
LAINIER AND JUNIOUS, WITH HIS MOTHER, DOROTHY

Lessons Learned

Age and Wisdom

I AM A PRODUCT of growing up in the northeast United States during segregation, but I did not realize that people were being separated by the color of their skin until I was much older. Since I did not know or understand why, I was not bothered by such segregation at that time. As a child, what I was bothered by was that I was born to an unmarried mother. I was considered by adults as illegitimate. I did not understand how a child could be illegal. I was frowned on as a child and criticized by adults who knew that information.

Well, as I grew into my teen years, that criticism disappeared from my mind as I learned to ignore such ignorance. I took the position of the famous Serenity Prayer: to learn to change the things I could, to accept the things that I could not change, and the wisdom to know the difference.

As I age, I am learning more about life. My opinions about matters may change once I experience different challenges for the first time.

I have learned to have intelligent conversations with myself. You see, I hear others' opinions about religion, politics, and life itself. We all have a different paradigm on which we base our opinions. If I am a product of my environment and my genetic makeup, then we are not all of the same mind!

My definition of success now is completing a goal daily. Yes, we can be successful at something every day! This means that we do not have to continue to chase an elusive success story, feeling like we never will attain our goals.

I conclude my journey for this book with a challenge for my family and readers: assess not only who you think I am but who you are!

This story is about life's unexpected changes that happened to an unexpected baby and his challenges becoming a man.

A teenager who lived life based on Einstein's quote, "Imagination is life's preview of coming attractions."

A boy who lived life confused until a defining moment changed his focus!

And a man who lives with his faith in God, regardless of the circumstances!

A story of a life lived not counting the number of breaths taken, but rather by counting the moments that can take your breath away!

CAREER PROGRESS CHART

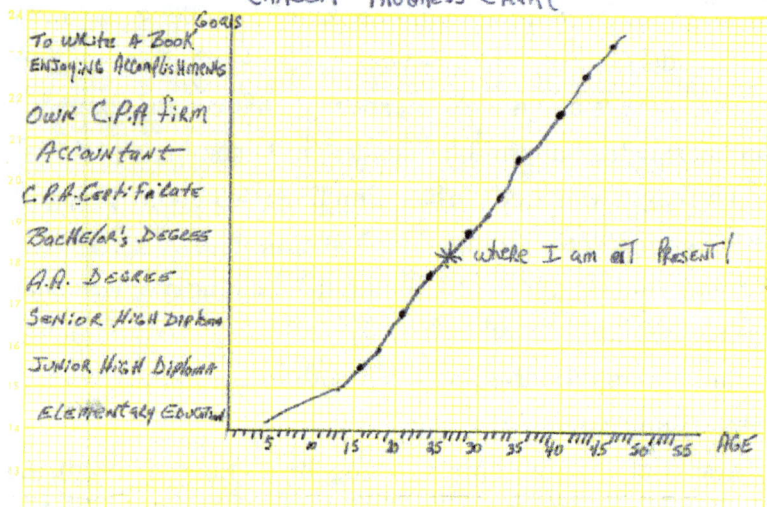

Goals

To WRITE A BOOK
ENJOYING ACCOMPLISHMENTS

OWN C.P.A FIRM

ACCOUNTANT

C.P.A Certificate

BACHELOR'S DEGREE

A.A. DEGREE

SENIOR HIGH DIPLOMA

JUNIOR HIGH DIPLOMA

ELEMENTARY EDUCATION

* where I am at PRESENT!

5 10 15 20 25 30 35 40 45 50 55 AGE

Life PROGRESS CHART

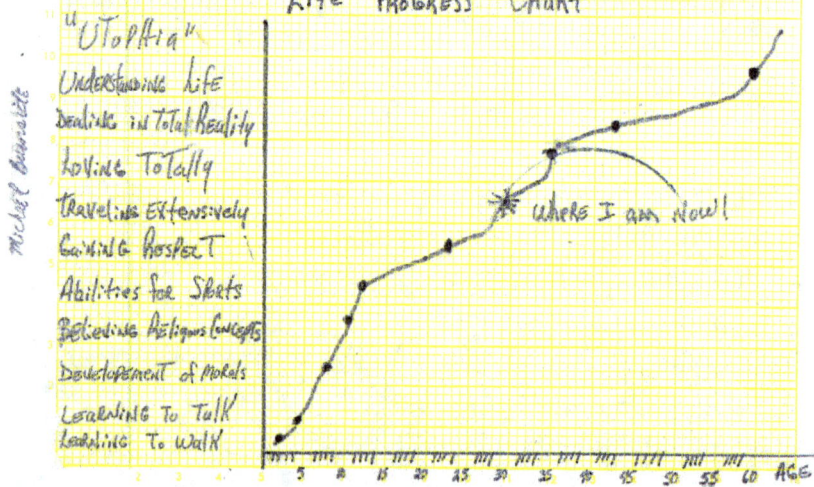

"UTOPIA"

UNDERSTANDING Life

Dealing in Total Reality

LOVING TOTALLY

TRAVELING EXTENSIVELY

GAINING RESPECT

Abilities for Sports

BELIEVING Religious Concepts

DEVELOPMENT of MORALS

LEARNING To Talk

LEARNING To WALK

* where I am NOW!

5 10 15 20 25 30 35 40 45 50 55 60 AGE

Michael Barnabite

BEFORE THERE WERE VISION BOARDS...

128

PS: Write It Down!

WHILE WORKING AS a statistician for the City of Baltimore under the mentorship of Mr. Quentin Lawson, I created this chart of milestones and goals for my career and life. I have kept this handwritten guide throughout all the years and moves since my twenties. This was an early version of a vision board, before I ever heard of a vision board, and maybe before anyone even talked about such a thing.

I am humbled, grateful, and, yes, thrilled to note that each of these goals has been achieved, including a top goal "to write a book."

Many people say there is power in writing down your goals. It certainly worked for me!

CHERYL BURNSIDE, 2024

Acknowledgments

THANK YOU TO my wife, Cheryl, for her encouragement and support throughout the process of writing this book. "It's time," she said.

Thank you to my daughter-in-law, Shalonda Burnside, for understanding my journey and summarizing this story as written on the back cover of this book!

Thank you to my sons and granddaughters, who inspire me to be my best!

Thank you to Cal and Joyce Beverly for their expertise in editing and guiding me through this process and to Heather Ward and Christine Holzmann for their help with design and photos.

And thank you to Marie Thomas, photographer extraordinaire, for capturing my story in the cover and author photos.

In addition to my family, mentors, and friends, thanks to all of the unknown people who helped shape me into a decent human being.

MICHAEL BURNSIDE, 2024

About the Author

MICHAEL BURNSIDE IS a lifelong accountant with an Associate and Bachelor of Science in Accounting and Finance.

He worked as an accountant with the city of Baltimore and the State of Maryland. He also worked as an accountant while free-lancing with various companies in Atlanta, Georgia. As an educator, he worked for thirty-seven years at Atlanta Technical College in the state of Georgia. Michael also owns Burnside Consulting, an accounting practice

Michael is a proud husband of forty-five years with his wife, Cheryl Burnside. He is a grateful father of two sons, Michael II and Wade, as well as a lovely daughter-in-law, Shalonda, and two wonderful granddaughters, London and Isabella.